A Journey To Becoming Your Own Best Friend

A Woman's Guide To Getting Out of Her Own Way

by Karen Chaston

Published by Kazand Investments Pty Ltd
Copyright © Karen Chaston 2014
All rights reserved
First Edition

This book is sold subject to the conditions that it shall not, by way of trade or otherwise, be lent, resold, hired out, or otherwise circulated without the publisher's prior consent in any form of binding or cover other than that in which it is published and without a similar condition including this condition being imposed on the subsequent publisher.

The moral rights of Karen Chaston has been asserted.

Cover illustration: Lace Cogan & Geoff Hupfeld
Editor: Lisa Wilder

Table of Contents

Forward	7
Acknowledgements	9
Introduction	17
Chapter One	29
The Contradictory Roles of Your Subconscious	
Chapter Two	49
From Merely Surviving to Thriving	
Chapter Three	63
Self-Esteem and Self-Confidence	
Chapter Four	81
The Energy of Women Collaborating	
Chapter Five	93
So what's getting in your way?	
Chapter Six	107
The Law of Dharma (Sanskrit for "Purpose in Life")	
Chapter Seven	125
Working Girl	
Chapter Eight	137

We're Here to Serve

Chapter Nine   **149**

The Essence of a Global Community

Afterword   **165**

References   **171**

About the Author   **175**

Forward

When I look objectively at the subject of "empowerment" of women there is an element within me that thinks it is absurd that we still have to highlight this item on the collective agenda. That half the population on the planet continues it's pursuit to balance the imbalance. Now we could easily lay the blame of women's lack of empowerment at the feet of men, but that is no longer useful or productive.

Instead like the pockets in many an era, the bra burning in the late sixties and seventies there is another renaissance occurring, a re-birth and flowering of female empowerment although this time around appears to lack the anger of other times. The resurgence of empowerment for women now has more of a sacred note in its call and not just the practicalities of equal pay and the right to vote.

Through this note, it calls us not to just change our psyches of why it is important for women to be empowered, but to change our hearts as well. That giving women a greater voice on our planet gives the planet new 'power' values that have typically been attributed to the feminine aspect i.e. compassion, support, nurture and encompassing.

So this is the nature of Karen's book; not just the 'how' but the 'why' female empowerment is important both individually and collectively. Recognising that our voice no longer needs to be loud but needs to have depth. Depth of understanding that a powerful woman is not just one who can play in a man's world but who can bring a new definition of powerful *to* the world.

So how do we do this? We start with the practicalities – voting for or backing ourselves, increasing our own pay rates, having our voice heard or taking a stand. For when we do so, we teach other women that they too can back themselves. That they can gain a sense of independence, financially, emotionally and maybe even spiritually. That we become our own guiding light in whatever world we find ourselves in.

Taking the journey of personal empowerment is not a selfish pursuit. In the context of women's empowerment, when one women breaks the glass ceiling she is taking all other women with her.

I encourage you, if we are able to take on the wonderful task of empowering yourself, not just for yourself and with all of its advantage but because the world needs women to show us that is can be done.

Jane Monica-Jones is an author and teacher in personal and professional development. Some of her books include – *Where'd My Mojo Go?!* and *The Billionaire Buddha* available on Amazon.

www.janemonicajones.com

Acknowledgements

*"At times our own light goes out and is rekindled by a spark from another person.
Each of us has cause to think with deep gratitude of those who have lighted the flame within us."*

~ *Albert Schweitzer*

This book would not have been possible without the love, friendship and assistance of so many people. I thank you all and am grateful that you are in my life, as you all continually assist me to become the person I came here to Be, to Create my prosperity and to Collaborate harmoniously.

To my book coach, Jane, thank you, thank you, thank you. Your knowledge and generosity is amazing. You provided me with the guidance so this book could be finalised in a couple of months. Totally **awesome**. Also thank you for writing the forward, you have captured so eloquently the essence of this book.

To my book editor, Lisa, thank you. You worked tirelessly so we could release this book. Thank you for all your fantastic work. The book flows so more easily thanks to your guidance.

To Andrew, my husband of 36+ years, thank you for allowing me to be me. I know at times it has not been easy for you. Even though at times you think I am *"bonkers,"* you've always been my biggest supporter, always by my side, never trying to make me be someone else.

To my boys, Ben and Josh, thank you for being amazing sons. I love and am proud of the men you have both become. You're living proof that boys *flourish* when brought up by a house-husband, which was very unusual in the '80s.

To Kim, my birth daughter, I love that you are in my life. I know that it has not been easy for you, and I thank you for continuing on this journey. Your birth was not the easiest, especially as I was so young and all alone as you entered this realm. In hindsight, it was a gift as I learnt that I can achieve anything alone, especially when I come from a place of love and desire.

To my beautiful friend of nearly 40 years, Kaz (Karen) Pearce, it is so nice that you are finally showing the world your true self, the person I first saw when we met as teenagers. Life and people made you hide your true self for a while, though thanks to BraveHeart Women, you're back, *"Dancing up a storm."* I love the fact that we share the same name as well as so many fantastic experiences together. Thank you for bringing the best out in me and sharing this journey. Also a special thanks to your amazing husband, Roger, for all his assistance and support.

To my Mum, Amelia, I know I came from love and am loved. Thank you for showing me that living your life worried about what everyone else thinks is not the way to live.

To my siblings, Chris, Pam, Jenny, Barb, Liz and Tony, I love you all and thank you for being a part of my life, for being there for all the good and the challenging times. For allowing me to be me, even when there was a lot of "verbal diarrhea" flowing. I am who I am today because of you all.

To all my in-laws, Alison, Peter, Cindy, John, Mark, Peter (Wack) and John, thank you all for assisting me to grow and share my life with you. Also thank you for being fantastic Aunts and Uncles to my boys, they love you all.

To my nieces and nephews, Buzz, Brendan, David, Laurie, Luke, Jas, Guy, Bianca, Troy, Dee, Craig, Jake, Zach, Alex, Ethan, Jess, Katie, Brett, Elissa and Adam, thank you for being in my life and for all the many great times we have had together. I can understand why I'm your favourite Aunt!!! Thank you also for being the best cousins to Ben Josh and Dan.

To all my friends over the years who have also been there for a lot of good and challenging times, Jillian, Denise, Rachel, Louise, Hup, Dommie, Jas, Heidi, Heidi & Heidi (yes, three Heidi's), Dale, Brian, Wendy, Anne, John, Roger, Richard and Alex, thank you.

To my special Manly Pacific friends, Carol, Sandra, Lisa, Plez, Trish and Priscilla, I love our quarterly catch-ups it is funny that we are closer now that we do not work together!!

To Lace, the most amazing graphic designer, thank you for designing the cover. Totally amazing, though more importantly thank you for reading the book and giving me such valuable feedback, which allowed me to write three more chapters with ease.

To Hup, yes I know I mentioned you earlier, though this is a special thank you for designing the illustration on the cover. It is all the more special that your artistic talents are part of this book.

To Dommie, yes a special thank you for creating my *"Karen"* caricature. I now have a signature for my books and blogs. Very special.

To Ellie Drake, the founder of BraveHeart Women,

thank you for your love, knowledge and guidance. Your generosity with everything has allowed me to write this book with ease. Thank you for being an example and continually assisting me to raise the bar.

To all my BraveHeart Sisters, thank you for your love, friendship and sisterhood. I love having you all in my life, though it would be remiss of me not to mention the ones who check up on me on a weekly basis – thank you Adrienne, Sarah, Kate, Dianne, Christy, Anita, Carol and Bela (Isabel).

To all the amazing women who have come into my life since I have been on the BraveHeart Women journey, Natalie, Marie-Jean, Dai, Jen, Tina, Deb, Nikki, Deb, Caroline, Maureen, Tracey, Elma, Fiona, Gloria, Sonia, Tara, Jacqui, Mardi, Kate, Nicola, Jeanette, and Sabhia, thank you for your love, friendship and guidance. You all saw things in me that at times I doubted were there. Apologies if I have missed anyone as this list is endless, you know who you are.

To my very special intuitive friend, Kim, I love having you in my life. I miss you when you travel. You are also a direct connection to Dan. Thank you. I am still not sure if you telling me something actually plants the seed in my mind so it becomes a reality or whether it was going to happen anyway. Either way works.

To my CEO group, Coraggio, John, CAB4 chair, Martin, and fellow members, Rod, Andrew, Robert, Sam, Andrew, John, Michelle, and Paul, thank you for assisting me to grow BraveHeart Women within Australia. I understand that most of you do not get it or me, though your ideas and feedback have assisted me greatly. A special thank you to Robert who looked me in the eye and said "You know you can write the book yourself, so just do it." You were obviously right!!

To Dan, my beautiful son who passed away July 2011, I miss you so much, though I am grateful for your guidance from the other side. I know you have given me BraveHeart Women, I feel you have me by the shoulders, pointing me in the direction toward becoming the person I came here to BE, thank you. You show me many signs on a daily basis that you are here with me, I am so grateful that I am AWARE so I can see these signs. This book has been written so easily because of you coming to me each night and guiding me. Again, thank you, you really do look after your Mum!!!

To my Dad, Jim, thank you for being you. I am who I am today mainly due to you being my father. At times I did not understand you, as you did not me. Though of all your children, I feel that I have most of your qualities. I look forward to you greeting me once I pass as you greeted and assisted Dan when he did.

To all my other relatives and friends who have passed, Nan, Ma, Fa-fa, Frank, Doreen, Eric, Toni, Stuart, Mike and all my uncles and aunts. Thank you for all the good times we had when you were in this realm and also for your guidance from the other side. I am so grateful for the way you all look after and guide me.

Introduction

*"Be who you are, say what you feel,
those who mind don't matter and those who matter don't mind."*

~ Dr. Seuss

Have you ever heard the saying, "There is only one person stopping you from achieving anything you desire in life"? While raising my three sons, I would say this to them all the time.

They would reply, "Is it Dad or you?"

I, of course, would say, "No, it's YOU."

It must have sunk in. Today, they are always joyous, prosperous and willing to try anything.

Unfortunately, I've noticed that a lot of women striving to create the life they desire are putting up barriers and making everything harder than it needs to be.

That is why I wrote this book—a guide to help women create the life they truly desire. We will step through the problems and limiting beliefs that get in our way and keep us stuck in a life that is unfulfilling, unrewarding, where we are unconscious to life. In a lot of cases, we are also stuck in a career that we did not even choose for ourselves.

This book is not for women who want facts, figures and a quick solution. This book is a journey to understanding what women are all about, taking away a better awareness of a woman's body on a bio-chemical and physiological level, as well as insight into why the "power of positive thinking" does not work for women.

We are exquisitely hardwired to fulfill a two-fold purpose:

- Connecting in meaningful ways, and

- Being authentically ourselves in relating to others and life around us.

We are all here to thrive. Unfortunately, many of us get stalled in survival mode, allowing perceived problems and limiting beliefs to run our subconscious mind. To succeed, it is not only essential to understand how our minds and bodies work. A critical step is to become OUR OWN BEST FRIENDS.

Meet Your Life Partner

You are the only person that you will spend your entire life with. So, why are you putting yourself last? Beating yourself up over silly things? And, in general, not looking after yourself personally, professionally, globally, and spiritually?

It was only a little while ago that this realisation came to me: *"You are the only person you will spend your entire life with."* I was in my mid-50s and I consider myself a really smart lady. I have a master's degree and am a CPA, so some people would agree that ticks a couple of boxes for being considered smart. So why did it take me more than 50 years to figure this out?

This phrase is really at the heart of the book. It is a stepping stone for you to take the journey to becoming your own best friend. Let's face it ladies, we go above and beyond for our best friend. We will never let her down. We have love, gratitude, and empathy for her. We have her best interests at heart, we're honest with her, and we are in harmony with her. Life is so much easier when she is around. We are connected and always present and conscious – totally in the moment – when she is around.

Why aren't we our own best friends too?

Many reasons that we give are universal: "It's selfish to put myself first." "I have a family to take care of." "A woman always puts herself last." I'm sure you can come up with many more, though in reality, like me, it has probably never really occurred to you that the best way to live our lives is by taking care of our own needs and requirements first. By doing this:

- We will be more fulfilled.

- We will have extra time and energy.

- We will come from a space of overflow.

- We will be a better wife, girlfriend, mother, sister, colleague, daughter—all of our relationships will be better!!

And from that space, we can give, give, give because we are all topped up; we are not running on empty and in resentment, thinking "When do I get to look after me? Have my time?"

The intention of this book is to guide you so you can start living your life as your own best friend. Just as recommended during the safety announcement on a plane, *"In the event of an emergency, the oxygen masks will come down. Make sure you put your mask on first before you assist others."*

Just the other day, I was in a health food shop really

enjoying looking at everything and the aroma of the candles. I commented to the 18-year-old sales assistant how much I love the shop, the products, the smells and how every cell of my body was tingling as it just loves being there ... knowing that there are good things coming to feed my cells. The young women replied, "Tell me about it, most of my wages go back to the owners as I also love the products."

"Good for you," I said. "You are the only person you will spend your entire life with and it's so great that you are looking after yourself at such a young age."

Her response was, "WOW, I have never heard that before. It makes sense. Thank you for making me aware of that, it changes everything."

And she was right. IT CHANGES EVERYTHING.

Most people are wanting or looking for three things in their lives:

- More time

- More money

- More quality relationships

The first step to achieving all three things is to become your own best friend.

Popping Your "Genie Bottle" Cork

I just loved the old TV sitcom "I Dream of Jeannie". How about you?

Just thinking about Jeannie takes me back to my childhood and how much fun I always had watching the show. Jeannie always managed to get Tony into so much trouble. Well, that is how it appeared then.

Now, as a more conscious adult, I am more aware that Jeannie was just being true to her authentic self. She was courageous; she remained TRUE to who she was, never changing to conform to anyone else's expectations, opinions or beliefs as to who she should BE or how she should act.

Jeannie lived her life in her *Essence*, always joyous. She always listened to her intuition and her heart, never allowing her brain to get in her way.

That is why people like us love Jeannie so much. We wanted to live life her way, not confined in our comfort zone allowing our FEAR to dictate the way we live, personally or professionally.

Maybe the show should have been called **"I Dream to BE like Jeannie"**.

Do you feel it's time to stop hiding and "pop the cork" on your "genie bottle" allowing your authentic self to come out?

The Essence of Collaborating

I realise now that my life purpose is to inspire as many women as possible to become their own best friend. When we come from that space, the next step will be women collaborating, truly collaborating from the heart without the mind.

Can you imagine what the world will be like when women are truly collaborating?

There will be no more need for the distorted feminine traits of judgement, competition, gossip and manipulation. These will be things of the past, because when you are your own best friend, you have self-esteem.

With self-esteem, we no longer require the distorted feminine traits. We are in our essence, we're being the person we came here to be, we self check all the time. We're continually asking ourselves: *"Why is this happening? What am I meant to learn here? What inside me needs to heal?"* We're continually looking for ways to grow.

Then when women start to collaborate and come from a space of ease, where we're no longer dis-eased, we will have made the first step toward creating harmony in the world.

As the Dali Lama said in 2009, *"The western women will save the world."* I firmly believe this will become a reality thanks to women learning how to become their own best friend.

It's a chain reaction, and the chain of events is:

1. Women become their own best friend. Women live in Ease.
2. Women collaborate through the Heart without the Mind.
3. Men notice how their life is in Ease (the old

adage "happy wife, happy life" is so true).
4. Everyone starts to come from a space of love, joy, gratitude and allowing.

This book will take us on a journey away from the "blame game," where we blame everyone except ourselves for everything that happens (or doesn't happen) in our life. The path we take will lead us toward becoming our own best friend, where we will be in essence. A place where we are consciously aware of everything around us. A place where we can create all the joy, prosperity and harmony in our life. Yes—the entire fulfillment that you desire.

This happened for me and I hope I can inspire you and others like us to empowerment, so we can have it all.

My Journey from Dis-Ease to Ease

Personally, less than two years ago, I was in a *groundhog* day life—eating too much, drinking too much, working too much. I did not even realise how dis-eased I was. I was so tapped into my masculine, always in fight mode, no wonder I was always tired, overweight and using stimulants to get through the day. I was so busy surviving, it's no wonder I wasn't thriving.

The funny thing is all of my friends and peers thought I was very successful and had it all, so to speak. I had the family, the career, the house, the car, overseas trips. I was actually paying more in taxes than most of my friends earned in total wages.

Even though I was very generous, in reality I was also wasting most of my money. This trait is very common among women. It was my way of not living up to my full potential. Unconsciously, wasting my money kept me even with my friends. In hindsight, that obviously makes no sense. After all, I started studying at age 38 to earn my Master's of Accounting and then my CPA, so why was I playing small?

With these qualifications, I was able to quickly rise to become a chief financial officer (CFO) of a publicly listed company. At the time, I thought, "Now I have found what I have been looking for my whole life."

I grew up in an era in which my parents' only desire for me was to grow up, be happy, get married and have children. I ticked off all those boxes by age 24. As much as I love my husband, children and the life we had, I was always looking for something else. Something was missing.

At the time, my soul searching misled me to think that the missing piece was "the successful career," hence the decision to formalise my higher education.

In hindsight (we are all so smart from this perspective), the successful career was just another path to me becoming my own best friend. Don't get me wrong. I loved my life as a CFO and I was really great at it and all my colleagues, peers, consultants and the stakeholders would agree.

Though as I said earlier, I was in a *ground-hog* day life, diseased and unaware of it. I did not realise how sick I was. Luckily, when my employer offered me a role in the new company, I had enough sense to realise I could not do the same job for less money, just because my titled changed. Though more importantly, I am sure there are many other women living a similar lifestyle and I would like to assist them and their employers to unlock their full potential.

So what changed? What happened to help me go from an unconscious, successful, dis-eased CFO to a woman who is her own best friend, a woman who is fully conscious, and in service to my fellow human beings, especially women?

Well, my friend, the answers to this question and many of your questions, lies in the following chapters. It's a journey in which we will find the answers to everything that may be getting in our way and holding us back from the life we so desire.

I promise you won't be the same at the end of the book as you are right now. You will be more conscious, inspired and passionate, with a clear path to begin your own journey.

Grab yourself a cup of tea or coffee, find a comfortable spot to claim for a while, tell your partner or family that it's "my time" and let's get started on the path to YOU becoming your own best friend.

Chapter One

The Contradictory Roles of Your Subconscious

"Honestly, sometimes I get really fed up of my subconscious - it's like it's got a mind of its own."

Alexei Sayle

A vital step on the journey to becoming your own best friend is to gain an understanding of the two directives of the subconscious mind.

The **primary directive** of the subconscious is our survival—to keep us safe. This is why we all have a comfort zone. I will go into great detail in the next chapter about the various survival patterns both men and women have developed, so we can easily identify our survival pattern. For now, here is a physiological generic description.

The subconscious manages the energies of our heart. It feels a sensory language of physiological sensations and emotional feelings, transmitted throughout our body's communication network.

When it feels we cannot handle an emotion, it takes over and puts us into protective mode – into survival. The majority of people live their lives in survival, not even consciously aware of it and more than likely when challenged on a certain trait they will say, "That is just my personality."

It's really important to recognise that *whilst you are in survival, you can't thrive.*

This brings me to the **secondary directive** of the subconscious—to ensure we thrive. That is right, we are not designed to merely survive. Even more compellingly, we're driven by inner motivational forces to thrive. This is why we are always searching for something else. And more than likely the main reason you are reading this book.

Let's explore in detail how the innate ability to keep us safe affects our lives when we are unconsciously stuck in survival mode and do not have the tools to combat it so we can begin to thrive.

Yes, the innate ability for SAFETY is the number one requirement in all women. It goes back to the start of time and it is ingrained in every single cell of our bodies.

Safety, the inherent or natural requirement, is what continually holds women back. To recognise this is huge, really HUGE. Awareness is the first step to change. *Awareness precedes action and we require action to change.*

So why is safety such a prevailing need in women?

Our Inherent Requirement for Safety

It really does go back to the time of the hunter-gather societies, when women did most of the gathering whilst men concentrated on big game hunting. According to some observers, hunter-gatherer women did not see this arrangement as oppressing since childcare was collective, with every baby having multiple mothers and male carers. The domestic sphere was not privatised but an empowering place to be.

This worked well for women who felt safe in the community. They found comfort in strength of numbers and worked collectively to fight any threat.

Personally, that would have worked well for me also. It's always great to share the jobs with everyone, instead of always getting stuck with the ones you don't like to do.

Also, having someone else to get up with the baby would be a blessing, especially after a big night. I guess they had 'big nights' even back then!!!

With today's high childcare fees, this communal approach to safety and caring for children might be a blessing, even a solution. Though once again, I feel I would be putting my hand up for going to work. How about you?

Ok, I know I have digressed, so back to the history lesson....

With social and technological innovations, the hunter-gatherer societies were displaced by agricultural and domestication, which led away from the egalitarian social ethos towards more patriarchal social structures.

Through domestication, it appears that women moved away from the community spirit of collaboration and more toward oppression. Women developed survival patterns in order to feel safe during perceived and real threats to their security.

We also live in a world now where it appears that the majority of media is based around keeping the population in FEAR, so there is constant reporting of threats to our safety – personally, financially, professionally and globally.

Whilst fear can be a symptom, the cause is the constant requirement for women to feel safe. This can be holding many women back from achieving their personal and professional goals.

There are many areas in which this shows up for women. As you read the different scenarios, make notes about which apply personally to you. Remember awareness is the first step to change. By becoming more conscious of how these survival traits hold us back, we can then take action and start to thrive. Start being your own best friend.

Our Lack of Voice in the Workplace

A constructive voice, when utilised effectively, will allow you to be recognised, rewarded and promoted in all aspects of your life.

There is really only one main reason why men are paid more than women and that is because they ask for more money. *They ask for it*, it's that simple.

Some women work very hard day after day thinking, "My boss will notice how great I am, always here on time, never sick, very efficient, so he will pay me what I'm worth."

Wow, how great would that be? Unfortunately, that is very rarely the case. Don't rely on merit or hard work to be the basis for pay rises.

We have to constantly show and inform our bosses how great we are and what an asset we are to the company. Men are constantly in their boss' face, telling them how the company could not survive without them, how much money they have saved the company and why they should be paid more money and promoted.

Let's be honest ladies, how many times have you had a boss who knew less than you, worked less efficiently than you and you wondered why the hell he had the job instead of you, especially seeing you were the reason he shined?

After learning in the mid-90s that a boss was taking credit for most of my work, and being paid *four* times what I was being paid, I made sure from then on that the right people were aware of who was doing what. Through self-promotion, I saw my yearly salary more than double over a period of a few years. This would never have happened if I sat back thinking, "They know how valuable I am."

Also, if I'm honest with myself, one of the main reasons (at the time) that I took redundancy (severance) from my CFO role (I am thankful everyday that I did) was that I felt my new boss would have taken credit for my work. I was past having people shine from my glow!!

Also, a lot of women hold back on sharing money-saving ideas as they feel they may be perceived as a trouble maker in the eyes of their employer. This is classic survival mode. What we are really thinking is "I need this job to survive," and we remain merely surviving instead of thriving.

Now don't get me wrong, I totally understand the thinking, "I can't rock the boat, I have a mortgage to pay. I can't survive without this job as I am living week to week."

Also, that way of thinking is "topsy-turvy thinking." It comes from a lack of self worth and self-esteem (which will be discussed in a later chapter) and is the reason we are trapped in a *ground-hog day* life, so to speak. .

By actually sharing our ideas with our bosses in a constructive, professional manner, they will more likely notice us, see that we care about the organisation, be thankful that they can save some money and, more importantly, may even promote us, especially if we continue to come up with these ideas.

In the early 90s, I was working at Dreamworld (a theme park on the Gold Coast in Australia) when the company went into receivership. During the first month, the receivers had a meeting with all 400 staff members. The first question they asked was: "If this was your company, what procedure or thing would you change/put in place in order to save money." By utilising the ideas from staff, the receivers immediately cut expenses by 30% and added a couple of new revenue streams.

From then on, I have utilised this way of thinking, constantly asking myself: "How can I do this more efficiently?" One of my pet hates when I questioned a procedure or process was to hear: "We have always done it this way."

I always managed to save expenses. As I was very efficient in my work, I always took on extra tasks and when I left a company; my role was normally replaced by 1.5 or 2 people to accomplish the same amount of work.

Start thinking and working from this perspective. Put your hand up for projects even if you feel that you may not have all the skills required for the tasks. You will learn quickly and grow exponentially when you are given the chance. And guess what? No one expects you to know it all. You just have to know where to look for answers and the internet is a valuable resource.

Richard Branson, founder of Virgin Group, is the first to admit that he is never the smartest person in any company meeting. He hires people to fill the gaps in his knowledge. A favourite quote of Richard's (and there are many) is: *"If someone offers you an amazing opportunity and you're not sure you can do it, say yes – then learn how to do it later."*

How much is your lack of voice in the workplace actually costing you (now and at retirement)?

In Australia, the statistics as of May 2014 show that of all taxpayers, only 2% of women ages 18 to 49 earn more than $100,000. Unbelievable isn't it? I was amazed when I read this.

The same data shows that the average weekly earnings are $1,516 per week or $78,822 annually. With superannuation at 9.5%, you're annually adding $7,488 to your super fund (retirement fund).

So let's do a little exercise now (I may be a *Recovering Accountant*, though I still love any excuse to use Excel). Take a look at what you could potentially have at retirement as an extra investment just by increasing your salary to $100,000, an easy salary to reach once you are part of the management team—and there is no reason you can't be a manager, remember *"If you can think it, you can do it."*

This table shows the yearly difference from the average weekly salary:

	Average	$100k	Difference
Base Weekly Salary	1,516	1,923	407
Annual	78,822	100,000	21,178
Tax	-17,164	-24,947	-7,783
Net Salary	61,658	75,053	13,395
Super (9.5%)	7,488	9,500	2,012

Now, if you invested the extra $13,395 on a monthly basis ($1,116 each month) over a 20-year period at a percentage yield of 10%, you would have **$847,456** at retirement.

Don't you just love compound interest!!

Even if the yield was 5%, you would have an extra $458,714.

Ok, I know that you may not invest the total $13,395 every year, but why not? If you have been managing without the extra income, why change?

Now, I am a great believer in the saying: "If all you do is save for a rainy day that is all you will get." I see this exercise as something completely different, as this is extra money you will be earning only because you have chosen to start to utilise your voice, to ask for what is rightfully yours.

Personally, I wish I had followed this advice when I had my CFO role. It totally makes sense, and just goes to show how dis-eased I was, not thinking clearly at all!!

Just imagine what your retirement lifestyle would be like

with an extra $847,456. Just think how much younger you'd be when you retire, how much fitter you'll be so you're able to travel and truly enjoy your golden years.

And the scenario above does not even account for any pay increases you would get over the 20 years or take into account your super fund. The extra superannuation of $2,012 per year alone will equate to an extra $128,000 at retirement if the yield is 10% (most super funds are averaging a lot more than 10%).
So the next time you decide to sit back, whilst working your "*arse off*" waiting for your boss to notice you and pay you what you're worth, think about this little exercise. You really are not doing "*your best friend*" any favours by not utilising your voice.

It is everyone's right to have a joyous, harmonious and prosperous life, so go and get it. Stop playing small. You know in your heart that you desire it because you deserve it. And your voice is the key.

The Way We Speak

The way you speak conveys a tremendous amount of information about who you are and how much value you have. Using your voice properly can help you hold attention, and make everyone listen to what you say.

Follow these simple guidelines to improve the way people respond to your voice.

- **Speak Low:** There is nothing worse than a nasally high-pitched voice. You need to find the lowest natural part of your speaking voice and emphasise that. Singers are often taught about singing from their belly, and you want to do the same thing. You want to be speaking from the chest and gut, which will sound lower and more resonant than speaking from your throat or head.

- **Speak Loud:** A male is not afraid of the sound of his own voice. He knows that what he is saying is worth listening to. Practice speaking, just a little louder than you're used to. Project your words so people can hear you easily.
- **Direct:** Try to eliminate "ums" and "ahs" from your diction, as these words make you sound uncertain and weak. Take a pause instead of saying these things.

- **Speak Slow:** When someone panics, they usually speak faster. They're in a rush, worried that they're not going to be able to say everything they want to say. What you must realise is that rushed speech communicates low value. Alpha, dominant males speak slowly. They know that they can take their time because people will listen. Therefore, slow down. Take your time, and trust that what you're saying is worth your audience's time. Be aware of the tendency most people have to speed up when they get nervous, and squash this habit. In fact, when you notice yourself getting nervous, feel free to just stop, take a deep breath, and then continue at a slower pace. It'll make you sound more in control, and that will help you feel more in control.

When it comes to your voice, follow these simple tips – loud, low, direct, and slow.

Fear of Owning Our Voice

A lot of women have a fear of owning their voice, based on a fear of criticism and oppression. By not speaking, we remain in our comfort zone. This is a major reason why some women have trouble saying no, which in turn leads to being overworked, exhausted, burnt out and, if we are honest, we are often taken advantage of, serving as other people's slaves.

We take on way too many things just so we are liked and not criticised. We fear that if we say what we think and feel, we will be ridiculed.

I was talking with Lace (don't you just love her name? Lace's response when you comment on her name *"There's nothing quite like it."*), an amazing young lady in her late 20s who just started her own graphic design business (she actually designed the cover for this book). Lace is newly married and I asked if she was going to have children in the future.

Lace said she was not sure. She has friends who have children and are *"stay-at-home mums"* and she could not see herself in that role, as she really wants to grow her business. She also mentioned that her friend's potential ridicule of her being a mum who places her child in day care was another deterrent.

As a mother of grown children and a woman who believes that we actually pick our parents so we can live the life we are destined to live, I asked Lace if I could give her some advice. Lace said "Yes, please."

My advice was this: "Lace, firstly, I realise you are

young and it takes a while to realise that what other people think of you and your choices in life is really none of your business. Secondly, to give birth and to raise a child is the #1 most rewarding and greatest achievement you can do in life and as a women it's even more special as you have the experience of carrying and experiencing your baby grow in your body, not to mention the actual birthing process. Thirdly, your child will have chosen you, knowing that you want to be a career-woman. He or she will know no difference, and they will thank you for being an example to them. And lastly, most of your friends will look at you and say, 'Wow, I wish I had the courage to live the life I want to live as opposed to the life that society thinks is correct.' "

Lace thanked me for the new perspective and said, "Yes, maybe children are in my future."

A lot of women hold back from doing the things they are passionate about because their so-called friends and partners say, "Why would you want to do that?"

Sometimes our profession is not of our choosing. How many times have you met someone who hates their job and they are only there due to "family tradition"? So sad. Recently I met Joe, a very successful lawyer in his 60s. He commented that he only went into law as that was what his father wanted, if he had his choice he would have been a musician.

Everyone is born to serve the world with their unique gifts. We are all unique. We add value and are valued when we become the person we came here to be. I wonder how many more fantastic songs the world would have if Joe had had the courage to stand up to his father and follow his passion.

Your voice is your unique gift; please allow it to be heard. Do not allow anyone to stop you from being you. Dr. Wayne Dyer, self-help author and motivational speaker, says it best:

"DON'T DIE WITH YOUR MUSIC STILL INSIDE YOU. LISTEN TO YOUR INTUITIVE INNER VOICE AND FIND WHAT PASSION STIRS YOUR SOUL. LISTEN TO THAT INNER VOICE, AND DON'T GET TO THE END OF YOUR LIFE AND SAY, 'WHAT IF MY WHOLE LIFE HAS BEEN WRONG?' "

Staying in an abusive relationship

Some women continually stay in abusive relationships and may even go back several times after leaving, which makes no sense to anyone except when we realise that she is fulfilling her innate ability for safety, in this relationship.

There are different types of abusive relationships, physical and mental abuse. Unfortunately, a mentally abusive relationship can do as much or more damage than a physical one as the scars can't always be seen by others.

Ok, agreed, it may not be ideal for the person to stay, though she knows exactly what to expect each day. Whereas, if she left the relationship it may be better or it may be worse, there is no guarantee, so she stays where she feels "safe".

Also, the unknown of how she will support herself and

her children keeps her there a lot longer than if she did not have children.

It is only when the situation escalates outside of her comfort zone and she no longer feels safe does she decide to leave the relationship. Unfortunately, this usually comes to pass when she has a greater fear—the safety of her children.

If you're in such a relationship, please read on, as the key to you leaving lies in you becoming your own best friend. Once that happens, you will be free and you'll have the courage and strength to live the life you came here to live.

FEAR

Fear is a vital response to physical and emotional danger, though often we fear situations that are far from life-or-death and thus hang back for no good reason.

More often than not, we use FEAR as the reason that we do not become the person we came here to BE.

Napoleon Hill, in the book *Think and Grow Rich,* states: "There are six basic fears, with some combination of which every human suffers at one time or another. These fears are named in the order of their most common appearance:

- The fear of poverty
- The fear of criticism
- The fear of ill health

- The fear of loss of love of someone

- The fear of old age

- The fear of death"

Personally, I look at fear from a different perspective, which is to use fear as a gauge so that when we feel FEAR we say to ourselves, "Ok, this is good. I am out of my comfort zone, so I must be growing."

I am not talking about a life-threatening situation. Of course, allow your fear to stop you from jumping out of that plane or off the cliff when you have a bungee rope attached to your legs.

I am talking about situations that stretch us out of our comfort zones. We need to be aware when survival fears, such as rejection, inadequacy or abandonment, surface and how they are holding us back.

I also came across this anagram as a great way to face fear (unfortunately I can't remember where so I can't provide a reference):

False

Evidence

Appearing

Real

How true it is.

Limiting Beliefs

The subconscious does not think on its own. It relies on our perceptions of events to know how to interpret life around us.

Most of our beliefs are generalisations about our past. They're based on our interpretations of painful and pleasurable experiences.

Unfortunately, most of us do not decide consciously what we will believe, so our beliefs are often misinterpretations of past events.

When our perceptions of life (our thoughts) activate survival fears, they produce a predictable pattern. Limiting beliefs produce images in our mind that cause fear-based emotions, which in turn activate our survival response.

Everyone has had limiting beliefs. Most of them we carry for most of our lives and are normally based from something that happened in childhood.

The moment we begin to honestly question our beliefs and the experiences we assign to them is the moment we start to replace the old disempowering beliefs with new beliefs that support the direction we want to go.

Like me writing this book. As I mentioned I was a CFO, an accountant, so I was obviously pretty good at math and English and writing were not really my favourite subjects at school. It's been a long time since I was at school, and recently I caught up with an old school friend. I mentioned that I was considering writing a book and that I actually thought I had at least three books brewing inside of me.

Her first reaction was, "Are you joking? You were hopeless at English. If anyone should write a book, it should be me?"

My response was, *"Yeh, I was not that good at English, though that was a long time ago. I've grown, written a lot of reports and essays during uni & my career, so all will be good and anyway that is why I also have a book editor."* I also reminded her that no one is stopping her from also writing a book.

For a long time, I did carry the limiting belief that I could not write. I got around this by realising that writing is just talking and I am really great at talking, so I can write. By now you may have noticed that this is my style and there is nothing wrong with that, it's just my *unique* style.

It's really good to think of limiting beliefs as a "set up" – a way of keeping us small, as they keep us focused on what we fear most: failing in life, or rather not being a success.

A study done years ago showed how people have limiting beliefs around valuing their worth. There were two identical job advertisements placed in a newspaper. The only difference between the two jobs was the salary. One listed a salary at $80,000 and the other at $200,000. Everything else was the same – all the skills, education, and tasks required were identical. I am sure you can imagine what happened.

That is right, the role valued at $200,000 received one-tenth of the applicants that the $80,000 role received. Why? Because people had limiting beliefs that they could not do a role valued at $200,000.

Powerful beliefs provide us with certainty that we can accomplish virtually anything. I love the saying *"You can think it, You can Do it."* This is a great philosophy for life. It's certainly mine.

I came across this little exercise (not sure where it came from) where you ask yourself seven questions so you can bust through any limiting beliefs.

- What is your most powerful limiting belief?

- How has this belief affected your life?
- How would your life be different without this belief?

- What is a new belief that you could consider? (Usually the complete opposite)

- How will your life improve with this new belief?

- In what way is the belief true?

- What can you accomplish with this new belief?

Try this next time you are aware of a limiting belief and let me know how it has worked for you by improving your life.

Chapter Two

From Merely Surviving to Thriving

"My mission in life is not merely to survive, but to thrive; and to do so with some passion, some compassion, some humor, and some style."

~ *Maya Angelou*

Becoming your best friend is the starting point to living a joyous, prosperous and harmonious life. In order to start to Thrive, we must understand that we have actually been in survival mode for most of our lives and these patterns have been running our subconscious minds.

We develop survival-based techniques, beliefs and patterns from the time we are born (some would argue from conception) up until around 8 years of age.

It is really important that you understand "they are not who you are," they are beliefs and patterns you developed to survive. And we can have a different survival pattern around different people and situations.

We can change our survival patterns around different people, though the majority of the time we each have a main default pattern.

The first step to cooling down our survival pattern is to recognise the components. Then we can start to identify the situations and people that trigger us into survival.

The aim here is to not play the "blame game." The aim is to cool it down, so that we go less and less into survival and more and more into thriving energy. When we're in our Essence, we thrive and from this space we can create the life we desire.

Just to be clear, everyone has a unique Essence that must be fed at a deep level. Understanding this essence can open up pathways to understanding yourself, your intuition and your own creativity.

I realise that there are many different communities that

can inspire people like us to live our life on purpose. For me, my own unique Essence blossomed once I started to fully embrace the BraveHeart Women Global Community.

The whole philosophy of the BraveHeart Women Global Community is for women to Be, Create and Collaborate.

1. To Be the person we came here to Be

2. To Create our prosperity with Ease

3. To Collaborate Harmoniously

When I first heard the following phrase, I got goosebumps and was filled with a 'knowing" that I had "come home" as I'd found something I had been looking for my whole life:

"The Mind of My Personal Purpose is free…It palpitates the Heart of My Professional Purpose, and at the Heart of My Professional Purpose is the Soul of My Global Purpose."

"I came here on this planet at this time to be a Woman who Blossoms and Creates so she can bring Harmony to humanity through her planetary wisdom to Collaborate."

In order for women to thrive, we have to come out of our survival patterns and embody thriving energy. In a later chapter, I will talk about how this is possible.

BraveHeart Women have categorised survival patterns into three default survival patterns. Remember, these patterns are not who you are, they are patterns developed for survival. Now that we're going to thrive, we no longer require these patterns and, in fact, they actually get in the way of our path to thriving. As we move into Thriving Energy, our survival patterns will no longer run our subconscious minds.

Before I describe the three main survival patterns, I need to explain the concepts of FIGHT, FLIGHT and FREEZE—the three primary physiological reactions when we are in survival mode.

We activate Fight or Flight when we believe there's a chance we can outrun or outfight our attackers (originally saber-tooth tigers). The Freeze response is activated when there is no hope (like a deer in headlights).

The Fight, Flight or Freeze responses begin in our body's autonomic nervous system (ANS), which is a network of nerve fibres extending throughout the body, connecting the brain with various organs and muscle groups. There are two branches of the ANS that work in harmony with each other to deal with the threats we face and then can recover from them.

- The **sympathetic** branch activates the Fight, Flight or Freeze response. This generates adrenaline so your heart beats faster, your muscles get tense, your eyes dilate and the mucous membranes dry up. This all allows you to fight harder, run faster, see better and breathe easier than you would without this systemic response.

- The **parasympathetic** branch activates the

relaxation response. It tells the body, "OK, you can relax now. The danger has passed. No need to be on alert anymore." Prompted by this message, the body's adrenaline subsides and you return to your normal physiological state.

Adrenaline, Cortisol and Oxytocin

FIGHT, FLIGHT or *FREEZE* are all states that BOOST adrenaline in the BODY. As women, we can't process adrenaline nearly as well as MEN. As a result, our bodies feel stressed and produce CORTISOL.

So that it is really clear, I'll explain a bit more about the bio-chemical reactions (natural hormones) that are produced in our bodies when we are either stressed or relaxed (in pleasure) and what happens to our bodies when these are produced in large doses.

When we go into Fight and Flight, the **sympathetic** branch of our autonomic nervous system activates, releasing adrenaline and cortisol into our bodies. So you can understand what affect this has on our bodies, think of a shark. Sharks are full of adrenaline.

Take a second to notice how your body reacts when you read, "Sharks are full of adrenaline." Your heart beats faster, you want to flee and your breathing changes—just by reading the word "shark".

Now you are more aware of what adrenaline does to your body. *Adrenaline* is a chemical that is produced naturally by the body. It helps regulate most of the important functions, such as heart rate, blood pressure and breathing. When we have a fright or have to fight or run, extra adrenaline is released into our blood. As this adrenaline circulates around the body, it makes our heart beat faster, helps us get more air into our lungs and increases the blood supply to the muscles.

Adrenaline was meant to be released in quick doses to support a Fight or Flight response that may be needed in a particular situation. It was not designed as a way of life, but there are a lot of people in the 21st century living 24/7 in this heightened state. No wonder so many of us are stressed, dis-eased, generally overweight and looking for quick fixes.

Cortisol (aka the stress hormone) is released in response to stress, sparing available glucose for the brain, generating new energy from stored reserves and diverting energy from lower-priority activities (such as the immune system) in order to survive immediate threats or prepare for exertion. However, prolonged cortisol secretion, which may be due to chronic stress or excessive secretion, causes significant physiological changes.

Cortisol lowers our metabolism, most often because cortisol is acidic and has a tendency to eat away at our organs when it is present in large quantities that we can't process. Instead, our bodies hold onto fat as a place to store the adrenaline and cortisol.

So ladies, we have to thank our FAT. I'm sure you never thought you would hear a woman say that!! Yes, thank our FAT for providing a place for the adrenaline and cortisol to be stored.

Oxytocin is a natural hormone that is secreted when the

parasympathetic branch activates.

It plays an important role in the neuroanatomy of intimacy, especially, in particular during and after childbirth, facilitating birth, maternal bonding and lactation.

Oxytocin has many nicknames: the love hormone, the bonding hormone, the ease hormone and the trust hormone. It is all of these things, and basically it has the opposite effect in our body as adrenaline.

Oxytocin reduces cortisol in the body and lowers blood pressure. It's also been known to improve digestion, which is often disturbed by high stress levels.

Dolphins are full of oxytocin. Yes, dolphins. Now, how does your body feel when you read "dolphins are full of oxytocin"?

Yes, amazing isn't it. A dolphin is always so joyous and playful with itself and with others. That is the way we want to feel ... that is what Essence feels like.

Three Survival Patterns

To discuss survival patterns, it's also important to understand the concept of *Feminine energy* & *Masculine energy*. They are different traits that are *both* inside every person, whether they are male or female.

Some examples of the survival traits of each are:

- **Feminine energy** – competition, manipulation, judgment, gossip

- **Masculine energy** – greed, need for control over others, need for power

Now, as I explain each of the three main survival patterns read carefully and take note of the examples so you can identify which survival pattern you have developed. Remember, *awareness precedes action.*

Survival Pattern #1

Feminine energy in FLIGHT
Masculine energy in FREEZE

This is the survival pattern seen in many everyday healers, for example. They came into this life believing that *if they "own" their voices, they would be oppressed, repressed, squashed or tortured.* A lot of this could be memory of past life experiences.

So a lot of healers came into this life not owning their feminine energy. They know they have it, but it's in FLIGHT because they are not owning it. They are afraid of masculine energy, be it their own or others', because it has squashed them in the past. So their masculine energy is in FREEZE.

People with Survival Pattern #1 also think they should give their gifts away for free. Basically, healers have an abundant amount of gifts to share, though they have a challenge creating prosperity.

So we can generally say Survival Pattern #1 has a challenge owning her voice and creating prosperity.

Now let's go on to Survival Pattern #3. Yes, I know I

have missed #2

Survival Pattern #3

Feminine energy in FREEZE
Masculine energy in FIGHT

This is the survival pattern for many of us who came into this life saying, "It really is not safe to be a woman, so what I am going to do is let my masculine energy lead as I feel I can survive with that more than I can with my feminine energy."

So many women who have had to survive in the corporate world utilised Survival Pattern #3 in order to compete, to get ahead (create), to survive. They put their feminine energy into FREEZE and tap into their masculine energy to succeed.

Similarly, many women who were part of the feminist movement of the 60s and 70s are actually in Survival Pattern #3. Survival Pattern #3, generally speaking, does not know how to COLLABORATE. She wants to, but does not know how because collaboration comes from feminine energy and her feminine energy is in FREEZE.

Sounds like many female CEOs I have met and a few politicians. What do you think?

And because she has her feminine energy in FREEZE, it gets in her way of being more, collaborating more and tapping into her deeper purpose.

For Survival Pattern #3, she knows what her role is but she does not know on a deeper level who her soul is, what her PURPOSE is.

Now let's look at Survival Pattern #2

Survival Pattern #2

Feminine energy in Flight
Masculine energy in FIGHT

Survival Pattern #2 came into the planet confused. *"I am not sure whether I should be #1 or #3 because I know on a visceral level I am attracted to #1, but on an intellectual level I am attracted to #3."*

"On a visceral level, I know I have a deeper level healing energy and I am here to support the shift of women collaborating on the planet, but it feels like I can't create prosperity in #1. So intellectually I'm attracted to #3 because I like how they get it done, how they make it happen and as I'm attracted to that so much, there's a conflict in me, between my intellect and my visceral space."

And that makes them a #2; they continually are vacillating between #1 and #2

None of these patterns are good. *THEY ARE SURVIVAL PATTERNS.*

Be more, Create more, Collaborate more

What is really interesting is that by taking the best of Survival Pattern #1 and the best of #3 and even the best of #2, I have learnt that I can BE more, CREATE more and COLLABORATE more.

So what is Be more anyway?

It is more than just a phrase. It is actually TO BE the highest expression of who you came here to BE.

What is CREATE more?

It is to create more with EASE as you're in your Essence.

And what is Collaborate more?

It's to learn how to COLLABORATE more for a harmonious planet.

Seeing I know that it is my purpose and I feel it is truly everyone's PURPOSE i.e. to heal our planet so we can harmoniously live together even with our disparate personal, cultural and religious beliefs.

Don't you feel we are done with *competition*, with a mindset of financial LACK, with a mindset of "what's in it for me" and with a mindset of survival?

Isn't it time for us to come into a space where there is more prosperity, neutrality, collaboration and thriving?

Intuitively, you will know what your survival pattern is. And you may have been one survival pattern at one time and another survival pattern at another time.

Remember, *this is not who you are as a human being.*
It is a survival pattern we are going to cool down as we come into *thriving energy.*

Someone may have been #1 but they could not produce prosperity so they forced themselves into #3, maybe the corporate world or as a politician or a high level job that's in competition in the world of masculine.

In Survival Pattern #3, we got burnt out, we felt like we had adrenal fatigue, we were exhausted, we thought that this is not the way we can go forward. We checked out on many levels, even emotionally, even at some level somewhat spiritually.

So we came back to survival #1, except in that pattern we can't create prosperity either so on some level our SOUL feels like it's in prison. We are oppressed and repressed, so much so that we actually feel *DEPRESSED*. So what do we do? We feed a multi-trillion dollar industry that feeds us pills or alcohol, we keep those industries alive.
So what is to be done? What do we do to change it?

We become aware of what survival pattern we have been in and then we allow ourselves to come out of it and into thriving energy.

Identifying Your Default Survival Pattern

Are you in Survival Pattern #1, afraid of owning your feminine energy because you feel it's not safe, so you allow yourself to remain invisible? Yet, at the same time you are not able to produce prosperity so you have guilt and shame around that and you would prefer to give everything away for free?

Are you in Survival Pattern #3, knowing that you do not want to be weak, you want to be strong, you want to produce, you want to make it happen? You want to make a difference and since it's perceived to be weak to be in ESSENCE in your feminine energy, you adapt and let your masculine energy lead? This is what we see in many people in the corporate world, politicians, doctors and attorneys. They came into Survival Pattern #3 knowing that this is not in true resonance with who they are as women.

Or...
Are you in Survival Pattern #2, still in that space of adrenaline because you keep going back and forth between #1 and #3? One day you want to give away all of your energy for free, certain that *"it's not about money"* and you do not want to create prosperity. Then, the next day you are sitting in a seminar about *"How to bring your competition to their knees in 24 hours."*

I mean, are you confused? Who wouldn't be?

Religion or spirituality?

Feminine or masculine?

Non-profit or for-profit?

We don't even know. (I say "we" because my survival pattern is #2.) So have you figured out which default survival pattern you've been unconsciously living your life?

No? Well, that is OK for now. Just keep reading. As we continue on this journey to you becoming your own best friend, you will work it out and then we can begin to cool it down, in order for you to come into *Thriving energy*.

Chapter Three

Self-Esteem and Self-Confidence

"Outstanding leaders go out of their way to boost the self-esteem of their personnel. If people believe in themselves, it's amazing what they can accomplish."

~ *Sam Walton (Walmart)*

Self-confidence and self-esteem are two very different things, and the aim in this journey is for us to have high positive self-esteem.

Basically, self-esteem is how we value ourselves. It is an essential requirement that is vital for us to thrive – to have normal healthy development. It is how we perceive our value to the world and to others.

Self-esteem affects our trust in others, our relationships, and our work – nearly every part of our lives. It arises automatically from within based upon a person's beliefs and consciousness.

Self esteem occurs in conjunction with a person's thoughts, behaviours, feelings and actions.

Psychologist Abraham Maslow's "hierarchy of needs" depicts self-esteem as one of the basic human motivations. Maslow suggests that people need both esteem from other people as well as inner self-respect. Both of these needs must be fulfilled in order for an individual to grow as a person and achieve self-actualisation.

Positive (high) self-esteem gives us the strength and flexibility to take charge of our lives and grow from our mistakes without the fear of rejection.

Women with high self-esteem will show up in their complete wholeness. It's doesn't necessarily mean they have it all together. They're not perfect. They allow themselves to know they're a whole human being with all their imperfections, knowing they still have much to learn, let go of and evolve into.

They are women who allow themselves to shine their light and show up in their full magnificence. Even though they don't know what it looks like, they know how it feels. Their ethos is: "I am not sure what I will be doing, though I want to show up."

Women with high self-esteem may or may not have self-confidence. Similarly, women with self-confidence may or may not have high self-esteem. Self-confidence is an outer focus of confidence. We gain confidence by being able to do something really well. A self-confident woman has to have all the skills and tools, all the nuances down pat, before she will go out into the world and display her skill. She gets her recognition from everyone else letting her know how great she performs a particular skill or task.

Low self-esteem is a debilitating condition that keeps individuals from realising their full potential because the person feels unworthy, incapable and incompetent. This quote (unknown author) sums it up eloquently: "If you put a small value on yourself, rest assured the world will not raise your price."

Here are some signs of low self-esteem:

- Negative view of life

- Perfectionist attitude

- Mistrusting others – even those who show signs of affection

- Blaming behaviour

- Fear of taking risks

- Feelings of being unloved and unlovable

- Dependence – letting others make decisions

- Fear of being ridiculed

Self-esteem can rise and fall throughout our lives if we are not strong in our belief of our value to the world. But we can tend to our self-esteem, like we would a garden, with daily bits of nourishment. I have a reminder on my computer screen saver. It has a beautiful white dove beside the words:

The strongest factor for success is self-esteem:

- Believing you can do it

- Believing you deserve it

- Believing you will get it

I also have a big sign on my wall that is shaped in a "U" says "JUST DO IT JUST BE IT", there is a gold frame copy of Andy Warhol's colourful $$$$ that sits at the top; so together it forms a circle - though that is another chapter!!

Low self-esteem comes from getting our self-worth from external sources, which then puts us into competition with everyone else. Just the other day, there were several articles about the low self-esteem of many celebrities.

The article stated: "It seems Mariah Carey's low self

esteem is a major factor in the split from her toy boy husband Nick Cannon." Most people would think that Mariah "has it all together." She is very confident when it comes to her singing and stage presence, though apparently she was not happy to share the limelight with her increasingly more popular husband.

Mariah and anyone with low self-esteem could embody this quote (unknown source) and then start to live their life accordingly: "So many people think you're awesome and special and worthwhile. Why would you listen to the one person who thinks you're not?"

When we truly love the person we are, we get our knowing and acceptance from within.

Creating High Self-Esteem

The BraveHeart Women global community philosophies and tools are all about creating self-esteem in women because it's from this space that we can "Be, Create and Collaborate" as women in harmony.

My intention here is not to talk about the BraveHeart Women tools, but to share ideas and some of my daily routines. I hope that you can use some of these ideas or think of others to create your own daily routine that will help you raise your self-esteem. It's a great start to becoming your own best friend.

Let's begin by reflecting on these questions:

1. How do you talk to yourself? Do you always use negative self talk?

2. Do you write in a gratitude journal?

3. Do you see your beauty through your own eyes? Can you look into a mirror without finding some fault with yourself? Can you stand naked in front of a full-length mirror without pulling a face? Have you ever listened to a love song, looking into your amazing eyes whilst singing the song to yourself?

4. Are you looking after yourself, with regular exercise and a healthy eating & drinking regime?

5. Do you meditate and love spending time alone?

We are going to look at these in detail, so you can start to consciously implement them on a daily basis. When you make these practices part of your daily life, you will be amazed at how quickly your life begins to change, and then you'll be well on the road to becoming your own best friend.

The way you speak to yourself.

Continual negative self-talk can make you depressed and ensure that your self-esteem remains low.

Just by catching yourself as you are about to say something negative to yourself and rephrasing it can make all the difference. Instead of saying "I made an idiotic mistake and I am hopeless at this job," rephrase it to "I made an error, though I can see where I went wrong so I will never make that mistake again. I know errors occur, and I can learn and grow from them."

Our subconscious does not understand negative words, so when we say something like "I do not want a boyfriend who treats me badly," it actually hears "I want a boyfriend who treats me badly." Hence, you continually get the same type of boyfriends who treat you badly. That is right, "different versions of the same loser."

Rephrase it by positively asking for what you want: "I want a boyfriend who treats me fantastically, one who loves me and will go above and beyond for me."

Also try and rephrase negative words as then your subconscious will create the positive. Instead of saying"this is difficult" say "this is not easy" and before long it will be easy.

A daily gratitude journal.

Most people concentrate on the negative things in their lives or all the things they wish they had. By creating a daily gratitude journal, we begin to flip that around and start seeing all the positives. Before too long, we really don't notice any of the negatives.

For this exercise, it's really important that you go out and buy yourself a beautiful hard-covered journal. This is something special for you, so spend a little more than you normally would. Even purchase a special pen if you like.

- Each day write down five things that you are grateful for in your life. Make sure that you try to have at least three different things each day, so you have to think about it.

- Try to evoke all your senses in your words: hear, see, smell and touch things, taste things, feel things. For example, you may choose to write something like: "I am so grateful that I live by the beach as I get to walk there every morning. I love to listen to the sound of the surf, feel the light breeze as I look at the sun, the clouds and the sky. I feel so alive just by experiencing the beach each day."

Beauty through your own eyes.

Begin each day by looking in the mirror and start to see the person that everyone else sees.

Stand there looking at who you are, look into your soul. Yes, you may have a few kilos to release (I say release as when they are gone we don't want them to find us again, so we release them forever) though look past them. See all the positive things, point out your uniqueness. Don't stand there comparing yourself to anyone else. You chose to be you, so honour yourself and start to recognise your greatness.

After a little while of doing this daily exercise, you will no longer see the extra kilos—you will go straight to the core of who you are. An amazing bonus is that you will actually start to release the extra weight because you stopped focusing on it.

Another very liberating exercise is to actually stand in front of a mirror naked. OK, I know you just said: "Naked, is she crazy?! No way could I do that." I said that the first time I heard it also, but just try it. You will be glad you did, and believe me; the kilos will be released a lot quicker and easier.

I also stand in front of a mirror, whilst I listen and sing along to a love song. You are singing the emotion of the song to yourself, so consciously realise this as you sing along. I have a few songs I do this with, though my favourite is "I Won't Give Up" by Jason Mraz

(https://www.youtube.com/watch?v=O1-4u9W-bns).

Let's take the time now, while you slowly read the words to the song, feeling each word, remembering that you are singing this love song to yourself...

When I look into your eyes
It's like watching the night sky
Or a beautiful sunrise
Well, there's so much they hold
And just like them old stars
I see that you've come so far
To be right where you are
How old is your soul?

Well, I won't give up on us
Even if the skies get rough
I'm giving you all my love
I'm still looking up

And when you're needing your space
To do some navigating
I'll be here patiently waiting
To see what you find

'Cause even the stars they burn
Some even fall to the earth

We've got a lot to learn
God knows we're worth it
No, I won't give up
I don't wanna be someone who walks away so easily

I'm here to stay and make the difference that I can make
Our differences they do a lot to teach us how to use
The tools and gifts we got, yeah, we got a lot at stake
And in the end, you're still my friend at least we did intend

For us to work we didn't break, we didn't burn
We had to learn how to bend without the world caving in
I had to learn what I've got, and what I'm not, and who I am

I won't give up on us
Even if the skies get rough
I'm giving you all my love
I'm still looking up, still looking up.

Well, I won't give up on us (no I'm not giving up)
God knows I'm tough enough (I am tough, I am loved)
We've got a lot to learn (we're alive, we are loved)
God knows we're worth it (and we're worth it)

I won't give up on us
Even if the skies get rough
I'm giving you all my love
I'm still looking up

Pretty powerful words aren't they?

Go and stand in front of a mirror and listen to this whilst looking into your own beautiful eyes. And yes, you are allowed to cry.

I recently attended a two-day training course in the city with my friend of nearly 40 years and fellow BraveHeart Women Resonator Kaz Pearce. We decided it would be easier if we stayed overnight in a hotel. In the morning, I said to Kaz, "OK, I am about to sing a love song to me. You go and stand in the bathroom mirror and do likewise."

Kaz has known for about a year that I do this daily, though for some reason she has not done it herself. After the song I said, "Isn't that amazing? How do you feel?" She replied, "I have never cried before by just looking into my own eyes, thank you."

Find your own love song; one that resonates with you, or use this one, it does not matter. What matters is that you do this each morning. Your day will be so much more, so much more and then, you will become so much more, so much more.

Regular exercise and a healthy eating & drinking regime.

I am not here to lecture you about the way you should be exercising, eating and drinking. Though I am here to remind you that *"**you are the only person you will spend your entire life with**"*, so why wouldn't you look after yourself?

I wish I had this advice when I started studying at 38. At the time, I was working at Dreamworld and my CFO boss suggested that I should go and get my "bit of paper", in other words my formal qualifications, which ended up being a Master of Accounting (thank you Peter, great advice).

I was the Financial Systems Manager and it totally made sense. I had teenage boys at the time and as we all know, they are more than happy if you are focusing on something other than them. Andrew, my husband (their dad), was happy to assist with extra work around the house.

So I took on two and one-half years of studying at Bond University on the Gold Coast (I love that university, the buildings are sandstone, amazing). I still had to work my 60+ hour week at Dreamworld, though that allowed me to have my four university contact hours during the day, at the university each week as I was doing two subjects a semester.

So with working, studying and some time with the family, I decided something had to go and unfortunately it was my gym time … yep, my exercise. That was my biggest mistake as at the time I did not understand what adrenaline, cortisol and using food and alcohol as a coping mechanism would do to my body. And on top of that, I was approaching 40!!

Anyway, for the next 15 years I carried around an extra 25 kilos than necessary. At the time of writing this, I have released 15 of these and will release the last 10 over the next few months.

So the best advice I can give you is to:

1. Follow a healthy eating regime, with plenty of greens

2. Exercise daily (aerobically four times per week), really get the heart pumping

3. Drink alcohol in moderation (4 drinks a week), drink green tea and plenty of water.

BraveHeart Women has created a salad we call "*The Blossom Salad*" as it keeps self judgment away. I eat this salad daily, sometimes twice (lunch & dinner). I have listed the ingredients below, except for the main ingredient – *LOVE.*

That is right, **Love.** As you're cutting up the ingredients, do so lovingly, thinking how great this is going to be for you and how every cell of your body will benefit from you eating this way. And guess what happens when you do this? The love and the nutrients go into the **HEART** of every cell of your body. So delicious!!!!

Also, make sure that you eat the salad without doing anything else. Don't sit in front of your computer or watch TV, just eat the salad enjoying every single mouthful, thinking, "*My body is so lucky receiving all this love and nutrients. No wonder I have so much extra energy.*"

Blossom Salad ingredients: small kale pieces, sliced tomatoes, pine nuts, chopped parsley, avocado slices, julienne cucumber slices, Himalayan sea salt, chopped cilantro, sprouts (any kind), extra virgin olive oil, and pinch of cayenne. For additional protein, add a small tin of tuna (in spring water) or quinoa (soak for 24 hours in order to sprout, then cook in boiling water for around 10 minutes). Enjoy!

Have your treats, though in moderation. Make sure that when you choose to have your treats *you enjoy them*. Don't start telling yourself, "I should not be eating this, blah, blah, blah." Instead think: "I am eating this and am enjoying this as I eat healthy and exercise regularly so this will not hurt me. I deserve this, my reward."

Meditation.

Meditating is an amazing way to start and finish each day. Meditation is really about training your mind to focus and concentrate.

There are many studies that show what happens to our brains when we meditate. The below explanation of what happens to each part of our brains is one of the better explanations I have found.

Frontal lobe
This is the most highly evolved part of the brain, responsible for reasoning, planning, emotions and self-conscious awareness. During meditation, the frontal cortex tends to go offline.

Parietal lobe

This part of the brain processes sensory information about the surrounding world, orienting you in time and space. During meditation, activity in the parietal lobe slows down.

Thalamus

The gatekeeper for the senses, this organ focuses your attention by funneling some sensory data deeper into the brain and stopping other signals in their tracks. Meditation reduces the flow of incoming information to a trickle.

Reticular formation
As the brain's sentry, this structure receives incoming stimuli and puts the brain on alert, ready to respond. Meditating dials back the arousal signal.

Now that we know what goes on inside our brains, let's look at some of the health benefits of meditation.

- **Better Focus:** When we meditate, we focus and this assists us to focus on things when we're not meditating.

- **Less Anxiety:** Meditation helps us look at things more rationally, therefore creating less anxiety.

- **More Creativity:** During meditation, we quiet our mind, which allows the creative juices to flow.

- **More Compassion:** Empathy and compassion are higher in people who meditate.

- **Better Memory**: Rapid memory recall is linked to meditation.

- **Less Stress:** Meditating lessens stress and can build up our brains and guard against information overload.

- **More Grey Matter:** People who mediate have more grey matter in their brains, which can lead to more positive emotions, longer-lasting emotional stability and heightened focus during daily life.

Personally, I have meditated for more than 10 years and I wish I'd started earlier in my life. I firmly believe the reason my salary increased over the years to $270,000 was through my daily meditation practice. Though meditation is not about increasing your salary ... it is a way for us to be joyous, prosperous and harmonious.

If you do not meditate, you may like to research some of the many, many different ways to meditate. Go online and find the one that suits you best.

Now you have a few daily tips for building your self-esteem, so you can become your own best friend. I guess the best way to end this chapter is with a quote from the guru, Buddha:

"You yourself, as much as anyone in the entire universe deserve your love and affection."

Chapter Four

The Energy of Women Collaborating

"What I love about collaborating is that you're working with other minds that work differently to yours."

~ Lauren Beukes (South African novelist)

You may have noticed that, at times, women can be a bit distorted with each other. We sometimes stray into the negative feminine qualities of judgement, competition, gossip and manipulation when we are together, either in a personal or professional situation.

This will only happen when the women involved do not have high self-esteem. When we have high self-esteem, there is no need for these distorted traits. When a woman has high self-esteem, "She knows who she is", "she realises there is enough for everyone", so competition and scarcity can become a thing of past.

That is right we move away from competition to Collaboration, from lack to Prosperity and from ego to Essence.

Collaborating, truly collaborating, with other women is the key to us creating harmony in the world. Achieving true collaboration, where the whole is definitely more than the mere sum of the individual parts, may not be easy. Though when the aim is creating harmony in our beautiful world, I am sure any obstacle can be overcome.

"The world will be saved by the western women," said the Dalai Lama in 2009. What he meant was that women inherently bring a greater focus on nurturing and connection, i.e. Love, which is the cure for the wounds of our time.

This is very true, though only when we move away from our ego and toward our Essence. Self-awareness and collaboration can help us get there.

To achieve collaboration, everyone has to have high self-esteem. Everyone has to set aside their ego, trust one another and share their expertise willingly.

I truly wish that I had been consciously aware of this when I was younger. How many times I have had fights with people just because they had a different opinion and/or my ego got in the way. When we are in our "knowing", there is no longer a requirement for us to force our opinions onto other people.

It is such a beautiful space to be in. We can just sit back thinking, "They are wrong and I know my opinion is right, though that is OK." It is not from a self-righteous or superior space, it is just from our knowing. We can simply allow others to have their views and sit back, neither agreeing nor disagreeing. This saves so much energy and time.

We can use that time and energy toward becoming our own best friend, so we can Be, Create and Collaborate.

Before I go into detail about the Essence of women collaborating, I am going to explain the other types of personal and professional relationships women have with each other.

Just to be clear, I am not talking about intimate relationships between women (not that there is anything wrong with that).

Attached Relationship

Have you ever felt like a friend or colleague is attached to you? This happens because there is something about you that they desire, crave or like. Perhaps you are attached to someone because of something you like in them. This is not healthy.

The subject of such attachment may feel the other person's energy even when they are not actually with them. They can drain your energy as well as draining their own.

I remember when I was working at Dreamworld; one of my staff members was like this. She would always make sure she sat next to me, had lunch at the same time and she even started dressing like me. That was not good at all.

I just could not really warm to her. At the time, I was not a BraveHeart Woman so I did not understand energy and how we are all connected and a reflection of each other. I was into my ego, so I actually saw this as a threat rather than a compliment.

Now, I am a great believer that I can only inspire women to empower themselves. I can't change them. It's a full-time job just changing myself!

If a similar situation happened today, I would suggest that she work on building her self-esteem and developing her own style. I would politely tell her to find her own space, as I will be releasing the attachment I feel in my space. (Thanks to the many BraveHeart Women tools, this can easily be done.)

It may feel good for the ego to have someone attached to you, but it's not good for either person's Essence. We need to release these women.

Remember, this is a relationship where one woman is attached to another. The "attacher" requires this to feel good about herself, though the other person does not want this relationship that is draining her energy and distracting her from being in her Essence.

Neither woman should want this unhealthy type of relationship. We won't need them if we are all our own best friends, embracing our uniqueness, truly in our Essence living a joyous, prosperous and harmonious life.

Co-Dependent Relationship

Most of us have experienced a co-dependent relationship. It is very common with a lot of women.

Both women show up, though they feel that for one to operate effectively they require the other person's skills. They need the other person so they can feel whole, and the other person feels the same way.

In the attached relationship, only one person wanted the attachment, whereas in the co-dependency relationship, both women want this relationship because they each take up one another's "skill shortage". For them to be individually effective, they feel they require this relationship to be effective.

While in a co-dependent relationship, we don't get to blossom into our own magnificence as we're always feeling the other person will handle our missing pieces. This gets in the way of our evolving and growing process.

Unfulfilled Relationship

An unfulfilled relationship is similar to a co-dependent relationship, yet distinctly different. It has a strong aspect of "You complete me. I am not whole without you." Though in this relationship, I don't require your skills to feel whole and competent.

More specifically, here my inner being is incomplete without you, though the relationship does not have a real sense of vitality. There are no delicious conversations or wisdom or healing. The vibrational frequency or energy of the relationship is always a void or a hole in it and that is the unfilled part—all the good stuff is being drained down the hole.

So to seal the hole, each person must become whole. And the first step toward this is to develop our self-esteem.

Controlling Relationship

A controlling relationship is where one woman is being controlled by another. The controller controls many aspects of the other person's being – what they say, what they do and who they think they are. This is not healthy at all.

What is interesting is that this relationship would never develop if the one being controlled had not invited the controller into her space. That is right; she needs this relationship so she can function.

The woman being controlled feels she is being loved, being given attention and sometimes they really love each other, though the controller feels she has to control.

The controller projects her own void, needs and fears onto the one being controlled, who welcomes this as they feel loved and they would rather be controlled than be abandoned.

This relationship stops both women from coming into their Essence. They would never become their own best friend as they feel they are each other's best friends. And this is not healthy at all.

Before I discuss the essence of female collaboration, I feel now is the time that we talk about empathy and sympathy, as it's really important that we as women understand the difference between these two feelings we have with other people.

Sympathy & Empathy

Please note that this definition has come from dictionary.com as I could not have explained it so eloquently.

Both empathy and sympathy are feelings concerning other people. Sympathy is literally 'feeling with' - compassion for or commiseration with another person.

Empathy, by contrast, is literally 'feeling into' - the ability to project one's personality into another person and more fully understand that person.

Sympathy derives from Latin and Greek words meaning 'having a fellow feeling'. The term empathy originated in psychology (translation of a German term, c. 1903) and has now come to mean the ability to imagine or project oneself into another person's position and experience all the sensations involved in that position. You feel empathy when you've "been there", and sympathy when you haven't.

Empathy can be employed as a communication skill. Empathy can allow great communicators to sense the emotions of an audience and is the mutual understanding and inspiration communicated to the audience. A lack of empathy involves a poor sense of communication that fails to understand the perspective of the audience. An audience may feel a positive or negative sympathy to both the communicator and the message as it is transmitted in communication. Empathy can also be found in the artist, musician, and drama, as well as the audience.

What is really important here to remember is that when we have sympathy, we become energetically involved; to take on the situation and this can last long after we have left the other person we were sympathising with. This is not good as we then become exhausted and waste a lot of energy on a situation that is beyond our scope of influence.

Empathy is the space we should be trying to come from as "feeling into" does not drain our energy.

The Essence of Female Collaboration

Collaboration between women is a beautiful relationship dynamic for women. This is the relationship dynamic all women must come into otherwise we will sabotage each other. This is the key to us creating a tipping point towards a more harmonious planet.

In this relationship two women show up in their complete wholeness. They do not have it all together. They are a whole human being even with all their imperfections, they have self-esteem and they know that they still have things to learn, to grow and with knowing all this, they are still ready to show up and shine their light.

"I want to show up, even though I don't know what it looks like..., I know what it feels like".

They are not necessary confident women though they are full of self esteem.

"I don't know what I'm doing though I do know who I am and the rest does not matter"

So the two women show up full of self esteem, they are whole and they both say:

"I am going to support the magnificence within you."

"So I'm complete, I'm competent that I will release what gets in my way on my own and I will give you space to evolve so that you will release on your own what gets in your way."

"We don't have to commiserate about stuff. We support each other's greatness (soul) not ego"

This is a beautiful relationship between women, they truly are their own best friends and because of this they can collaborate, as they have moved from *Ego* to *Essence*.

And because of this relationship, the two women standing side by side, both 100%, 100% in their Essence a 3rd energy is created and that is the *Energy of Collaboration.*

Each woman realising this; *"My focus is on the energy within me of letting go and evolving. And by doing that I am contributing to the energy of the 3rd energy, The Energy of Collaboration"*

It's about evolving together and growing together. And once women start to come from that space… our planet will come into harmony. Yes we can collaborate harmoniously.

More importantly the world will be; as best described in this passage from *"Align, Expand and Succeed"* (a compilation of stories by Christine Kloser, Lynne Klippel, Michael Port, which I highly recommend you read).

"The old models of fierce competition, profits at all costs and unethical business practices are falling away. The new paradigm of business, which we call conscious business focuses on collaboration, authenticity serving consumers with heart and contributing to the healing of the planet.

When you consciously choose to use eco-friendly products, negotiate business deals with integrity or focus on solutions that benefit everyone, you are acting as a conscious business person.

The world you dream of, the business you dream of, the impact you dream of having are all there for you. We feel the keys for you to discover that world and thrive in it for the rest of your days.

It is truly about creating a new world for generations to come. Conscious entrepreneurs letting your heart and soul guide your business along with your knowledge and expertise. As we become more awake and conscious of the greater good in our individual business endeavours we will create a better world.

When you align with who you truly are, and expand your presence in the world... success naturally flows in abundance to you. And this is the journey of shifting the paradigm of entrepreneurial success."

Yes ladies, the key to this world starts with us becoming our own best friend. So let's continue on our journey, so we can BE CREATE and COLLABORATE.

It's up to us to be the change we wish for the world....

Chapter Five

So what's getting in your way?

"I am not what happened to me; I am what I choose to become."

~ *Carl Jung*

As I mentioned earlier, there is no point playing the *'blame game'* if we do not have the life that we desire. The place to look is actually inside of ourselves. We must take stock of who we are and what barriers we are putting up, and then we can start to look at ways we can begin to become the person we so truly desire to be.

Women, more so than men, tend to blame everyone except themselves for what is happening or not happening in their lives. Does any of this sound familiar? "If only I was born to the right family, if only I could find the right man instead of continually dating the same 'loser', if only I had more time, if only I was smarter." The list can be endless.

My mum, Amelia, would always say to me: "'If' *is such a small word, though it can mean the world to you, if you let it.*" Yes mum, I was listening!!

At BraveHeart Women, we refer to the things that get in our way and stop us from achieving as our 'Buts'. We have actually created a way to release our Buts. It's called *"DYBO (Dance Your Buts Off)... It's not the Butts you sit on; it's the Buts you live in."* We all have them at some point: "But I don't have enough money," "But I don't have enough time," "But I don't know where to start"... *But, But, But!!!*

We have talked about survival patterns, self-esteem and the energy of collaborating, so now let's look at some of the *'if's'* and *'buts'* that may be getting in our way. Things that are holding us back from shining our light and becoming our own best friends.

The Blame Game

The blame game is one of the most common barriers that get in our way and one of the easiest to identify and change.

It is really easy to look at our current life and blame everyone except ourselves. The very talented actress Katharine Hepburn sums it up beautifully: *"We are taught you must blame your father, your sisters, your brothers, the school, the teachers – but never blame yourself. It's never your fault. But it's always your fault, because if you wanted to change you're the one who has got to change."*

When we look at our life as a choice, and everything that happens to us as a learning experience, the sooner we will start to change.

The fact you are reading this book is a great first step for you to realise that everything in your life is a result of the choices you make. The sooner you start investing in yourself the sooner you will start to *be* the change. Everything in life is a choice.

I am continually looking inside when something happens, so much so that I ask myself: *"Why am I creating this, what am I meant to learn here, how can I grow from this?"*

The good thing is we will always learn more from a negative than we ever will from a positive. Also, the negative will pass a lot quicker the more we look at events from this perspective.

A personal, really great example of how a negative can turn into a positive when we use this way of looking at events is my redundancy (layoff) from my CFO role.

Briefly, two companies were being merged together by the new owners and I was to have a role, though not as CFO. The role offered to me was at a lower rate of pay, even though I would be doing more or less exactly the same things I was doing in the old company, so I decided to take redundancy.

Initially, when I received the contract offering less money, I went into my EGO: "How dare they?! I have worked here for 5 years; they know what a great asset I am." But within a couple of hours, I started to look at this as an opportunity for a new start.

Within days I started to feel that something completely different was about to happen. I started to come out of the *'ground-hog day spell'* I was under (though I didn't realise it at the time) as I began to look at things from a different perspective.

At the time, Richard, a friend and former boss (different company) said to me, "I have a feeling that you are about to embark on something completely left field and I think it has nothing to do with accounting." I replied, "I know, I have the same feeling, wonder what it will be?"

It only took a couple of weeks and I knew exactly what my new direction was to be, and I am grateful everyday for the low salary package that was offered to me, otherwise I may still be in my *groundhog daze*, as opposed to being a BraveHeart Woman.

I even went back and thanked my old boss for not fighting for me and for offering me a lower salary. At first he thought I was being sarcastic (one of my survival pattern traits), though very quickly he saw I was being genuine. He was glad I had taken the time to thank him as up until then he had thought maybe he could have done more.

Firstly, if I did not have high self-esteem, I would have accepted the role. I knew that there was no way that I could have stayed there for less money. It would have eaten me from the inside out. And there is no way to THRIVE when we are in that sort of survival!!

I have always known that I am here for a special purpose. I now know that I am here to serve women, to inspire them to empower themselves. I have always had a voice though, up until now, never the message. So now my voice is very happy and the best thing is that I am in service. A giver's gain philosophy: By giving to women what they want, I will get what I want and that is to be joyous, prosperous and harmonious.

All during my management career, women would come to me and ask me to help them get a pay rise. I would assist, though I could never understand why they just could not go and ask for it. I always felt, *"Well if they said no, I am no worse off, though they may say yes, so I could be heaps better off."*

To be honest, it really annoyed the crap out of me that they could not see that for themselves. Now of course, I understand these women. I understand that it's all just part of their survival. I am so glad that I can now assist them to come out of survival into thriving.

Yep, my voice is happy!!

The Value of Giving a 'No'

One of the major reasons women burn out and have very little time for *what inspires us* is that we take on too many things. This is mainly because we do not know how to say no, perhaps because we want to please everyone. This does not work. We end up totally exhausted with so many misaligned relationships and projects—all because we cannot say **NO**.

Social psychologist Susan Newman, PhD, author of *The Book of No* sums up nicely the differences between men and women when it comes to saying NO.

Men are expected to assert themselves and speak their mind; that's what gives them status in our society. They learn to say no early on because if they don't, they're labeled wimps. On the other hand, women earn praise for playing nice and co-operating. As girls, we're singled out for being helpful. This manifests in adulthood as an eagerness to please and gain others' approval, typically by agreeing to assist anyone who asks. In fact, the female need to please is so ingrained that many chicks equate saying no with saying "I don't care about you."

To counteract our socialisation toward helping others to the detriment of ourselves, let's look at some great reasons to say No. Eventually this will become second nature to you, and you will begin to see that you not only have more time and energy, you are also more content.

- **Time:** There are only 24 hours in the day and how we use it makes a difference. There are no refunds if you waste the time. If you are spending a lot of your time helping everyone else with their relationships and projects, it takes away from time you could invest in creating your own unique life.

- **Resentment:** If you are continually doing things for others and not yourself, you will have resentment and wonder, "What about me, when is it my time?" This is a big energy waster and leaves you feeling flat and depressed.

- **Exhausted**: This naturally continues on from time and resentment. If you are always too tired from doing things for everyone else and being resentful, how will you have the energy to create the life you desire?

- **Continually being asked**: This is a bit of a snowball effect. When people know that you can't say no, they will continually ask you to help, as this allows them extra time to create the life they desire!!

- **Not doing your friend any favours:** That is right, if you are continually there to help, how are they learning and growing? Growth is what we are all required to do and it's through doing things ourselves that we grow and learn.

As you start to say no, keep in mind that you do not need to give a reason why you can't do something. This is the biggest trap we fall into. Giving a reason allows others to alter their request to fit in around your reason for saying NO. Keep it simple, just say NO.

A good guide for any request is to ask yourself this question: **"DOES THIS REQUEST MAKE ME FEEL**

EXCITED OR FURTHER MY GOALS?" AND If the answer is no, then say **NO.** It really is that simple.

The Value of a Receiving a 'No'

A lot of women have trouble coping when someone says no to them. They take it personally, especially if the no comes to them on a professional basis – from asking for a promotion or in a sales environment.

But you can view a "no" as an opportunity to grow. Remember, we will always learn more from a perceived negative situation than we ever will from a positive situation.

Also, when we take things personally we can waste a lot of time and energy worrying about it as opposed to quickly asking ourselves, *"What am I meant to learn here, how can I grow from this experience?"*

A couple of things to think about when you receive your next NO are:

- A NO helps us remain humble and grow.

- See a NO as an opportunity to expand and heal. As it integrates inside of you, then you'll get to share with others so we all grow and evolve.

- Receive the NO with elegance. Be elegant – don't get depressed or mad or shut down or run away. Elegance is to tenderly and humbly and somewhat joyously be in the moment.

- The No allows for an opportunity for many

YES's based on synchronicity, based on You getting WISER, and then everything in your life aligns even more.

Women Learning How to Receive

Some women cannot even receive a compliment

Yes, women give, give and give to the point of exhaustion and then they have a hard time receiving. Some of us can't even receive a compliment without downplaying it, "What, this old thing?" "Yes, I lost a bit of weight, though I still have to lose some more."

Now ladies, let's look at this in detail. First, do you realise how rude that is? The person has taken the time to compliment you and really all we have to do is say *'thank you'* (even if we don't agree). That is right, look them in the eyes and say *'thank you'*.

It is so rewarding to just say Thank You. We know deep down that the compliment we received is warranted, otherwise they would not have said it. Just own it, no need for us to play small. Just say thank you.

And then everyone is happy, the complimentor (one giving) is happy, as their time was not wasted and the complimentee (one receiving) is happy as something has been recognised by others. Not that we are seeking recognition, remember our recognition comes from within; we have self-esteem, though it is always nice to have external acknowledgement now and then.

I am a great believer in giving compliments even if I do not know the person. Just the other day I was in a coffee shop talking with a friend when a lady walked in wearing a dress that just made her shine. She looked amazing. I excused myself from the conversation and as the lady walked past me, I said, "Excuse me that dress looks amazing on you, really makes you shine."

The lady was a bit taken back at first, and then she said "Thank you so much, you have made my day. Up until now, it has not been going very well, and now it can only get better." See what happens when the giving and receiving is done with love and respect. My intention was pure and it was received that way.

Our reluctance to freely receive affects all our relationships – with other people and with other things we would like to receive in our lives; namely our relationship with money.

Your Relationship with Money

Our ability to create the income we desire comes down to our relationship with money. If we believe we do not deserve to create or earn a certain income, than that is exactly what will happen. As I keep saying," *if you can think it, you can do (create) it*" and this works both ways. If we feel and think we are only meant to live in poverty, than that is exactly what our life will bring us

Like everything else, money is a form of energy that is attracted to energy that is like itself. Our relationship with anything determines how much of that thing we are attracting or repelling.

Money does not exist by itself. It is always attached with the energy of the person who relates to it. The same money can be experienced by different people in different ways according to the relationship they each have with it.

Rich people know that money is important, that is why they have it. Some poor people think money is evil, they have to become aggressive or pushy to earn it and that is why they lack it.

Our relationship with money is an imprint from early childhood. It comes from the way our parents would talk and act in regards to lack or prosperity.

Think back to what you were told or overheard in regards to money. Were you told *"money is evil"* or *"money does not grow on trees"* or *"a lot of millionaires create their first million illegally and then grow their millions from that space"*? Sometimes, hearing our parents always fighting over money can leave an imprint.

Personally, in the early 1980s, I can remember watching *"To the Manor Born"*, an English sitcom about a person born to the manor. There were several classic lines which I thought were funny, though thinking back this highlighted my poor relationship with money. Here are a couple of quotes so you can see what I mean:

- "No one ever makes a million honestly! Then he squandered it on loose women, then he made another million or two: all very seedy."

- "If you want to know what God thinks of money, just look at the people he gives it to."

The aim here is to have a healthy relationship with

money, one where you know that money is important and you appreciate it, though you are not attached to it. Remember the classic line *"what you appreciate, appreciates in value and what you don't appreciate, depreciates in value"*. That is classic accounting 101 (I know, give me a break, remember I did say I was a *recovering accountant*)!!!

The biggest way we can improve our relationship with money is to see it as fuel that we are earning so we can create so we can give back. It is just an energy exchange for our efforts, a state of being where we are whole and doing what brings us joy.

We really do have to *love money*. That is right, we have to *accept, understand, respect and appreciate* it, just as we do with any other relationship in our life. That is the key to creating a joyous, prosperous and harmonious life.

Though if our ideas for making money come from fear, anger or the need to prove ourselves, then money will never bring us happiness. Look around at how many millionaires in the world seem to have had this motivation for making their wealth. Yes, in this case they may have a lot of money, though they would not say they are joyous or prosperous. Many seem to be always fighting to protect what they have, never trusting anyone.

Personally, now I know that I love money, I have a great relationship with it and I accept it, understand the energy flow, as well as respecting and appreciating money. I always say that *"one of my biggest delights will be to always turn left on a plane"*. For those of you who do not understand my analogy, just think about when you enter a plane, everyone turns right except for business or first class they all turn left I hope we can share the experience together sometime.

I love this quote from Oprah: *"Be thankful for what you have; you'll end up having more. If you concentrate on what you don't have, you will never, ever have enough."*

I guess the best way to end this chapter is to reiterate that giving and receiving are different aspects of the flow of energy in the universe. And in our willingness to give that which we seek, we keep the abundance of the universe circulating in our lives.

I found this beautiful daily commitment (unknown):
- Wherever I go, and whomever I encounter, I will bring them a gift. The gift may be a compliment, a flower, or a prayer. Today, I will give something to everyone I come into contact with, and so I will begin the process of circulating joy, wealth and affluence in my life and in the lives of others.

- Today I will gratefully receive all the gifts that life has to offer me. I will receive the gifts of nature: sunlight and the sound of birds singing, or spring showers or the first snow of winter. I will also be open to receiving from others, whether it be in the form of a material gift, money, a compliment or a prayer.

- I will make a commitment to keep wealth circulating in my life by giving and receiving life's most precious gifts: the gifts of caring, affection, appreciation and love. Each time I meet someone, I will silently wish them happiness, joy and laughter.

What a beautiful way to live each day.

Chapter Six

The Law of Dharma
(Sanskrit for "Purpose in Life")

*"The '**Law of Dharma**' says that we have taken manifestation in physical form to fulfill a purpose. The field of pure potentiality is divinity in its essence, and the divine takes human form to fulfill a purpose."*

~ Deepak Chopra, *The Seven Spiritual Laws of Success*

It is so beautiful to realise that we are all actually here to fulfill a purpose. When I was younger, I always thought we were here to just have fun. That was certainly how I lived my life. The reason I stayed 14 years working at Dreamworld was because it was so much fun. I can remember saying once, "We're not really here to entertain the guests. We are here to entertain each other." And we did.

Even now, when I get together with my old Dreamworld buddies we have so many laughs, you know the ones, deep belly laughs where you end up crying, your side begins to ache and you nearly pee your pants. So hilarious, just thinking about it makes me smile. I could write a book just about the antics we all got up to, though I better honour the code: "Whatever happened at Dreamworld stays at Dreamworld."

Eventually, I did grow up and become conscious. It is nice to know now that we actually have three purposes to fulfill: A Personal Purpose, A Professional Purpose and a Global Purpose.

This chapter and the next couple will explore how we can begin to discover our different purposes. This is a journey within our journey, as we become more aware you will know. To be honest you already know, you just may not be aware of them at this stage.

In this chapter, we'll discuss the concept of your personal purpose. First, let's have a lesson or a review of the *Laws of the Universe*.

The Laws of the Universe

We are all *spiritual beings having an earthly experience*. So, it is always good as we journey through life, and especially while on the road to becoming our own best friends, to be consciously aware of the *Laws of the Universe*.

It is also great to realise that everyone faces struggles and challenges, especially when we decide to step up and become the person we came here to be. These challenges are just the universe testing us to see if we are serious, we're not just trying to *fake it till we make it*. The universe wants to make sure we have taken the leap, *The Leap of Faith*, so to speak.

On the back of my business cards, I have this saying: "*She took a leap and built wings, she then began to soar and soar, because she became a BraveHeart Woman.*"

There are 12 universal laws. I have seen them written in numerous publications, though one of my favourites is from Milanovich and McCunes book *The Light Shall Set You Free* (1998), so here is an excerpt:

1. **The Law of Divine Oneness** The first out of the 12 universal Laws helps us to understand that we live in a world where everything is connected to everything else. Everything we do, say, think and believe affects others and the universe around us.

2. **The Law of Vibration** This Law states that everything in the universe moves, vibrates, and travels in circular patterns. The same principles of vibration in the physical world apply to our thoughts, feelings, desires, and wills in the etheric world. Each sound, thing, and even thought has

its own vibrational frequency, unique unto itself.

3. **The Law of Action** The Law of Action must be applied in order for us to manifest things on earth. Therefore, we must engage in actions that support our thoughts, dreams, emotions and words.

4. **The Law of Correspondence** This Law states that the principles or laws of physics that explain the physical world – energy, Light, vibration, and motion – have their corresponding principles in the etheric or universe. "As above, so below."

5. **The Law of Cause and Effect** This Law states that nothing happens by chance or outside the Universal Laws. Every action has a reaction or consequence and we "reap what we have sown."

6. **The Law of Compensation** This Law is the Law of Cause and Effect applied to blessings and abundance that are provided for us. The visible effects of our deeds are given to us in gifts, money, inheritances, friendships, and blessings.

7. **The Law of Attraction** This Law demonstrates how we create the things, events, and people that come into our lives. Our thoughts, feelings, words, and actions produce energies which, in turn, attract like energies. Negative energies attract negative energies and positive energies attract positive energies.

8. **The Law of Perpetual Transmutation of Energy** This 8 out of the 12 Universal Laws is a powerful one. It states that all persons have within

them the power to change the conditions in their lives. Higher vibrations consume and transform lower ones; thus, each of us can change the energies in our lives by understanding the Universal Laws and applying the principles in such a way as to effect change.

9. **The Law of Relativity** This Law states that each person will receive a series of problems (Tests of Initiation) for the purpose of strengthening the Light within. We must consider each of these tests to be a challenge and remain connected to our hearts when proceeding to solve the problems. This law also teaches us to compare our problems to others' problems and put everything into its proper perspective. No matter how bad we perceive our situation to be, there is always someone who is in a worse position. It is all relative.

10. **The Law of Polarity** This Law states that everything is on a continuum and has an opposite. We can suppress and transform undesirable thoughts by concentrating on the opposite pole. It is the law of mental vibrations.

11. **The Law of Rhythm** This Law states that everything vibrates and moves to certain rhythms. These rhythms establish seasons, cycles, stages of development, and patterns. Each cycle reflects the regularity of God's universe. Masters know how to rise above negative parts of a cycle by never getting too excited or allowing negative things to penetrate their consciousness.

12. The Law of Gender This last law of the 12 Universal Laws states that everything has its masculine (yang) and feminine (yin) principles, and that these are the basis for all creation. The spiritual Initiate must balance the masculine and feminine energies within herself or himself to become a Master and a true co-creator with God.

Your Personal Purpose

In *Seven Spiritual Signs of Success,* Deepak Chopra shared the following story:

From the age of four, my children heard that there was a reason why they were here, and they had to find out what that reason was for themselves. I taught them to meditate at the same age, and I told them that I never ever wanted them to worry about making a living.

If you're unable to make a living when you grow up, I'll provide for you, so don't worry about that. I don't want you to focus on doing well in school. I don't want you to focus on getting the best grades or going to the best colleges. What I really want you to focus on is asking yourself how you can serve humanity and asking yourself what your unique talents are. Because you have a unique talent that no one else has, and you have a special way of expressing that talent and no one else has it.

They ended up going to the best schools, getting the best grades and even in college, they are unique in that they are financially self-sufficient, because they are focused on what they are here to give.

Do you resonate with that? I do. I feel that it's the most

beautiful and sanest way to bring up your children. I really do highly recommend you read the book. It is a treasure and each spiritual sign is designed as a way for us to live each day, each week ... that is why there are seven.

We all know in our hearts that this is the way we should live our lives, the way we should bring up our children. Yet what happens? What gets in our way? Some would say life, though in reality there are many things, distorted things that get in our way and it all starts or has a foundation in FEAR.

I know that I have discussed FEAR in an earlier chapter, though I would just briefly like to reiterate how disabling fear can be, if you allow it to be. That is right, we have a choice and the sooner we realise that everyone has fear (yes everyone, no matter who they are), every time we step out of our comfort zones onto unfamiliar territory. Fear is just part of growing and stretching.

But, there are many other negative emotions that can get in the way of us becoming our own best friends as they cause us to be miserable and sad. The emotions which can become negative are *hate, anger, jealousy and sadness*. These emotions can make us dislike ourselves and others, and take away our confidence.

Negative emotions can dampen our enthusiasm for life, depending on how long we let them affect us and the way we choose to express them.

These four negative emotions are the basis for us not finding our Personal Purpose. They get in our way and stop us from thinking and behaving rationally and seeing situations in their true perspective.

When this occurs, we tend to see only what we want to see and remember only what we want to remember. This only prolongs the anger or grief and prevents us from enjoying life.

The longer this goes on, the more entrenched the problem becomes. Dealing with negative emotions inappropriately can also be harmful, such as expressing anger with violence.

At BraveHeart Women, we refer to emotions as *"energy in motion"*. Emotions are psychological (what we think) and biological (what we feel). Our brain responds to our thoughts by releasing hormones and chemicals that send us into a state of arousal. All emotions come about in this way, whether positive or negative.

We at BraveHeart Women believe that everyone's personal purpose is to *"Blossom into the person they came here to BE"*. So, we can see how holding onto the negative emotions of hate, anger, jealousy and sadness, can stop us from *Blossoming*.

Now I would like to go through the various stages of life and point out some of the good things each stage brings when we are *Blossoming*. The main reason for doing this is that we may be stuck in our negative emotions, comparing ourselves with other people. This can keep us stuck in our emotions, stopping us from blossoming.

Maybe now might be a time to get yourself another cuppa (coffee or tea), as it's time to have an honest conversation or look at yourself. Blossoming really does come down to developing high self-esteem, as when we have this there really is no requirement for hate, anger, jealousy or sadness.

We will look at everyone else from a space of Love. Always glad that they have achieved whatever they have, that they can stand and shine their light, and that they are joyous, prosperous and harmonious.

In Australia, we have what is called the *"Tall Poppy Syndrome"*. Basically, this is a social phenomenon, in which people of genuine merit are resented, attacked, cut down, or criticised because their talents or achievements elevate them above or distinguish them from their peers.

Not that long ago I was told that the Tall Poppy Syndrome dates back to our convict settler years. The story goes:

"The convicts were shipped from England to settle the colony. The English soldiers could not chain the convicts up as the convicts had to work and clear the land. So they told the convicts that if they chose to run away they would not chase them, though every convict that was left behind would be beaten because you ran away. So when a convict stood up to run away all the other convicts would jump on him and drag him down, as they did not want to be beaten."

Not sure if this story is true though it does make sense as to why we have a Tall Poppy Syndrome.

Personally, this is keeping us from all standing tall, declaring our space and showing the world our unique gifts. I will not allow this syndrome to stop me from shining my light.

How about you?

Your Relationship with Your Mother

Now, my intention here is not to devalue your relationship with your father, as it is very important, though as women it is really extra special that we realise the exceptional bond we have with our mothers and all the other maternal fore-bearers back about seven generations.

As I mentioned earlier, my mother, Amelia, has seven children and she also had 20 grandchildren. My mum actually gave birth to eight children though her first daughter, Gail, was strangled at birth by the umbilical cord.

My maternal grandmother, Ethel (Ma), had six children and 26 grandchildren. She was an amazing woman who lived until she was 91. Ma came from solid stock; she was always busy and could cook up a storm. Ma outlived all of her children except for my mum.

Unfortunately, I understand firsthand the heartache my mother and grandmother experienced at losing a child. Dan, my son, passed away in 2011, at age 27.

To understand with empathy, the lives your maternal ancestors have lived are the key to women collaborating. Women for centuries have lived unfulfilled lives. For generations, women have been seen as "house-wives" and that was the only role we should fill.

Whilst at times I do not understand my mother and the things she does, I know in my heart that she has always wanted the best for me and my siblings. She is glad that things have changed and I can become a successful entrepreneur, so I can live a joyous, prosperous and harmonious life. Something she would have loved for herself, as did Ma.

If you don't have a great relationship with your mother, change your perspective. Start to look at her life with different glasses. You may then begin to develop a beautiful loving and caring relationship. You really will be glad you took the time to see things differently.

The Teenage Years

As we all know, the teenage years can really be the best of times and the worst of times. As teens, we really do care about what other people think and if we have a particular skill or talent we gain confidence from excelling at it. And also, our talents can bring out the negative emotions in our friends and peers, which in turn can create a few insecurities in other areas of our lives.

At this stage we're looking outside of ourselves to find what we are missing, not realising that we should be looking internally as that is where the answers we are seeking lie.

I grew up in a large family—six girls and one boy. The boy is the baby. We still call him the golden child!! I was the third eldest and, at times, it was not the easiest family to live in. Mum says, "There was always someone in that house with PMS." Sounds funny, though it was true.

At 16, I found myself pregnant. Now before I dated the father of my baby daughter, I was briefly with a guy and he dumped me because I would not have sex with him. Needless to say, I was not going to let that happen again.

Now, I could easily say that I wish I had the courage to say No, but then my daughter Kim would never have been born. I adopted Kim out, though I've been lucky to have her in my life now. I really love the person I am today and I also know that I am the sum of all of my experiences, so I realise I was that person for that very reason.

So if you are a teenager reading this, embrace the teenage years, look for love from within, don't take yourself too seriously, have fun, be responsible and choose a career that makes you want to leap out of bed each morning, as then you know you're on purpose.

And if you are an adult woman reading this, love who you were as a teenager, this was your grounding for becoming your own best friend.

Remember Deepak's advice from earlier in this chapter.

Your Single Years

I have purposely titled this "Your single years" as this can go on for a few years (decades) and they are all about loving and embracing who You are. You should be getting everything from yourself. When you're getting everything from yourself, you will then be a complete or whole person. Then when you are whole, you will find that you will attract other whole people into your life, be it a boyfriend or friend, as well as all the opportunities, adventures and everything else you desire.

If you are single, look at all the benefits of being single (and there are many), don't dwell on the negatives (remember there is a ying & yang in everything). Don't compare your life to your married friend's life. When we go into the *"comparison game"*, the distorted emotions arise in us and our friends. Own your decisions and your choices. You are you and they are they.

I have seen this referred to as "frenvy" or friend-envy. "A little bit of jealousy isn't a bad thing and if harnessed right, it can be beneficial to a woman's internal and external growth."

Remember what we see of their life is just our perception. We don't really know what happens behind closed doors. We all put on armour to protect ourselves, especially if we are potentially living a life that we may not have chosen knowing what we know now.

So if this is the case, now is the time to change it. It really is up to you.

Your Married Years

We get married for various reasons. I trust that your marriage is a long and happy one; this will certainly be the case if you had your self-esteem intact when you walked down the aisle. Also if we walked down the aisle for the marriage and not just the wedding!!

Look at all the joyous things in your life and don't compare your life to your single friends or any other married couple. You have grown beyond the 'single & carefree' person you once were, you have made a commitment to move on.

Life is good just where we are, if we choose to see it that way.

The Parent Years

Now these years are forever, though here I am referring to when we are actively looking after our children, bringing them up. I always say "that as much as kids make a marriage, they can also break one." These can be trying times and we can lose who we are for a while if we allow this to happen.

For a while, life is a big *ground hog* day of baby food, sleep, runny noses & poop, though when we look back they do go quickly. This time more than any other time is when we should live our life, our way, our family way and do not compare our life to anyone else or any other family.

This is the key to our blossoming at any stage, though very much so now.

Single life can look attractive now and then, though we know in our hearts this is our purpose and we are right on track.

The key is to make sure you make time *"for you"*, *"for you and your husband"*, *"for you"*, *"for you and the kids"*, *"for you"*, *"for you, your husband and the kids"*, *"for you and friends"* and also *"for you."*

Remember that you are the only one you will spend your entire life with, so you deserve to BLOSSOM, no matter what stage you are at in your life.

The Empty Nest Years

These times can be the most rewarding or the most challenging. And the difference comes when we have lived the former years on Purpose.

If we've lost ourselves during our lives being there for everyone else except us and don't really know who we are, the empty nest years can be very challenging. The good news is: It's never too late to blossom.
Now we're aware of this ... it's time to take action.

Should have been "XYZ" by now

These years can come all through our life. This is when we or society has put certain expectations of whom or at what stage we should be by a certain age.
This really is ridiculous and a classic example of people projecting their life onto us as well as comparing ourselves to others.

Some examples of this are:

- I am nearly 30 and single; I can't believe I don't even have a boyfriend. I should be married with two kids by now.

- You're dating, oh when are you getting engaged?

- You're engaged, oh when are you getting married?

- You're married, oh when are you going to have kids?

- You have a child, oh when will you have another?

- You have a child; surely you will be a stay-at-home mum (or go to work)?

- You have six kids, oh surely you will stop now?\

It goes on and on. Our family, friends, and colleagues think they are being loving and caring when they say these things, though they are actually projecting their views of life's stages onto us.

Wouldn't it be nice if the conversations changed to:

- I love who I am, single and nearly 30. I will attract my ideal partner now. My self-esteem is high.

- You're dating, are you in love, does he make you feel safe, does he allow you to be you? Great, I look forward to you getting engaged and married if you feel its right.

- You're married; do you feel you would like to have kids?

- You have a child, isn't it great that it's your choice to either stay-at-home or work?

So what's stopping you from Blossoming?

If for some reason you are looking at your life and you're not happy, well now you have the awareness to change it. Awareness precedes action. And action is the key to you living your life on Purpose. Our Personal Purpose is to Blossom into the Person we came here to BE.

The 12 Laws of the Universe are here to assist you in blossoming. Read these often, especially when you are feeling life has taken you down a wrong path. They assist us to realise it's just a different path, not the wrong one. Also, please remember the most powerful law **#8**. Here it is again:
"The Law of Perpetual Transmutation of Energy. It states that all persons have within them the power to change the conditions in their lives. Higher vibrations consume and transform lower ones; thus, each of us can change the energies in our lives by understanding the Universal Laws and applying the principles in such a way as to effect change."

Though before we continue our journey so you can discover your Professional Purpose, here is a *"Personal Purpose"* thought-provoking prose by Karen Salmansohn (best-selling self-help author).

"You Gotta Look for

The Good in the Bad

The Happy in the Sad

The Gain in your Pain

And What makes you Grateful not Hateful."

Remember that you are the only one you will spend your entire life with, so you deserve to BLOSSOM, at every stage of your life.

Chapter Seven

Working Girl

"You're the first woman I've seen at one of these things that dresses like a woman, not like a woman thinks a man would dress if he was a woman."

Jack Trainer (played by actor Harrison Ford in "Working Girl", 1988)

Now let's have a look at your Professional Purpose and the things that get in your way, stop you from creating with Ease.

Do you sometimes feel *YOU* personally have been lost in your race to the top? Or are you looking at the women ahead of you saying to yourself, "Hmm, if that is who I have to become in order to have that role, maybe I should re-think my career goals, and start my own business."

Personally, I can relate to both. I am the first to admit that I lost myself the further I rose in my corporate roles. I did mimic a male-oriented style and was always in my Fight pattern. It has taken me a long time (longer than I expected) since leaving my CFO role to return to a space in which I embrace and embody my feminine qualities.

I remember when I started my CFO role, I wrote an email to one of our bank managers. I started it off the usual way, "Hello Daniel, I hope you are well", and closed it with "Have a great weekend, Kind Regards Karen". I cc'd the CEO into the email. Within seconds of hitting send, the CEO was in my office stating, "Karen, great email except for the start and the ending. We have a professional relationship with the bank; they are not your friends." From then on, I started each email with just the person's name, without the *Hi, Hello or Dear*. I would never ask anything personal or say *Have a great weekend*. I was business, business, and business focused.

At the time, I loved it. It was snappy and quick. Now, of course, I look back and I cringe. It may seem insignificant by itself, but it was representative of how I really did lose "me' in the process. Sure, I was highly regarded by my peers, colleagues and all the stakeholders, to which I say, "BIG DEAL. Karen, you should have courageously continued to be you. Your aptitude would have been noticed along with your courage!!!!!!"

Everyone has to pick their battles at work, and if your boss gives you a direct order, it may be prudent to follow it. But in cases where there is wiggle room, think of what you really want to do, not what you think the boss wants you to do.

Courage is really the key to fulfilling our life purpose and truly creating everything we desire. To be honest and authentic as a leader is a sign of strength. Yes, you are making yourself vulnerable – but you are also willing to be open and show your true personality and colours.

I firmly believe that whilst we all have a choice, our business education and the workplace tend to squash our innate feminine qualities of empathy, nurturing and collaboration.

Women in leadership positions find themselves with an identity dilemma: If we act like a typical male leader, we are perceived as 'hard' or 'cold' because the behaviour jars with that of the stereotypical woman. If we act like typical women, we are perceived as less effective, because the typically male personality traits are still considered more effective.

During the last couple of years, I've met with many men who "champion women". They are really keen to see women succeed with their true self intact. Initially they were excited to be working with women CEOs and interested to see how the extra-added value of a woman's *natural innate qualities* could enhance the organisation leadership style.

Unfortunately most of these men who championed women reported experiences similar to this, as ....:

These women were impossible to work with. It appeared that they had to continually prove themselves, never trusting anyone, always acting as though someone was out to get them or plotting to bring them done. With this mindset, the women made sure their colleagues and subordinates were the first to fall; belittling them in front of others, creating unrealistic deadlines, setting up camps and pitting one employee against the other. In general it was a very unpleasant and un-collaborative environment.

So whether you are thinking about continuing on your journey up the corporate ladder or down the road toward entrepreneurship, let's have a look where it may lead you.

The Best Person for the Job

A lot of research now suggests that the kinds of skills women have are very desirable for the C-suites of the future. This will mean men and women can embrace their own unique styles, instead of forcing themselves to fit into the prevailing model.

A 2013 Ernst & Young report states that businesses need to change their mindset about gender equality if they want to fully harness the financial benefits of having a diverse workforce.

"From both a social justice perspective and from a practical standpoint of wanting the best person for the job, I think it's frankly ridiculous that we only appoint senior people from 49 per cent of the population," Coco-Cola Amatil chairman David Gonski said.

Whilst other studies indicate that women could actually make better leaders than men, when not forced to adopt a traditionally 'male' style, sacrificing their own natural instincts in the process. Personally, I believe there should be a balanced board.

Men and women complement each other's gifts and skills and the company will be more profitable when these differences are embraced. The main differences between men and women are:

- Our brains are wired for different things
- Woman communicate differently
- Woman problem solve differently
- Woman negotiate differently
- Woman think about the future differently

The Cost to the Corporate Bottom Line with Low Female Representation

In 2011, the Australian-based Reibey Institute found ASX500 companies with women directors delivered significantly higher return on equity (ROE) than those companies without any women on their boards. Specifically:

- 6.7 percent higher over a three-year period

- 8.7 percent higher over a five-year period.

The 2010 Insync Surveys: "Gender Agenda: Unlocking the power of diversity in the boardroom" found that members of gender-diverse boards believe that they:

- add more organisational value through the quality of their decision making

- have Chairs that are more effective in several ways

- have directors who act with greater integrity

- are more vigilant about the connection between management's remuneration packages and performance

- require better documentation of roles and responsibilities.

Yet even with all this empirical information, in Australia we still have only 18.2% of women represented on ASX200 boards (*the Australian Institute of Company of directors*). And the new appointments since 2010 appear to be in decline each year:

- 56 women appointed in 2010

- 68 women appointed in 2011

- 41 women appointed in 2012

- 37 women appointed in 2013

- 31 women appointed in 2014.

Whilst I understand that there are numerous reasons for this low representation (as discussed in earlier chapters), some women view corporations today as fundamentally flawed and limiting in their value structures, with "office politics" being stated as the driving factor for women leaving corporations to start their own businesses.

This is certainly the case in Australia where we have quite a unique situation, with the highest educated women as a percentage of population and the least amount of women in senior management and board positions.

Women Entrepreneurs

With the cost of starting a business at an all-time low, women are saying *"no thank you"* to spending years climbing and clawing their way up the corporate ladder, dealing with corporate politics, and working long days without feeling the overall fulfillment they crave.

The glass ceiling that once limited a woman's career path has paved a new road toward business ownership, where women can utilise their sharp business acumen while building strong family ties.

Many women start businesses that align with personal values and offers freedom and flexibility when it comes to things like scheduling. The high cost of child-minding has prompted a lot of young mothers to look for other ways to supplement the family income.

There are many added benefits to owning and running your own business, though we need to make sure that road leads to the *Holy Grail* and not to a *Hellish Nightmare*.

More than 80% of businesses fail in the first 18 months and 50% in the first 5 years. Some of the issues behind these stats are:

1. **Buying a job instead of a business.** Yes, initially we are the business and do all the roles. Though quickly, we should build the business and take on employees so that we are very rarely hands on, and instead spend the majority of our day "working *on* the business instead of *in* it."

2. **Thinking too small.** A lot of people just want to be their own boss and create a wage for themselves and nothing else. Instead aim to build a business with profit and employees.

3. **Not having enough capital.** The business will always take a lot longer than planned to take off and generate income. So have enough capital in reserves for twice amount of the initial time planned. Initially as the only employee, we may need to be Jill-of-all-trades. But there are only 24 hours in the day and we have to allow for time for ourselves. Just because we were a senior manager in a company, it does not mean that we are skilled in every aspect of running a company.

4. **Competing on price alone.** The profit in your business comes after all expenses. Some people count all the revenue coming in without considering the costs associated with each

revenue stream. We may be better off doing fewer jobs with a lower cost associated with each, rather than more jobs with higher costs. Know your margins!!

5. **If it isn't working, change it.** Don't keep doing the same things for no results. Test and measure everything you do, keep adjusting and adjusting until you get the desired results.

6. **Not having a business coach.** No matter how large the company, the best CEOs has business coaches. We need to have a sounding board and, most of the time; it cannot be the board of directors or your employees. Through the business coach, you will learn and grow and will be able to make the tough decisions when required.

There are numerous other reasons, but enough of the pitfalls. Just remember, *Awareness Precedes Action* and *You will always learn more from a negative, if you choose to look at the lessons you have learnt.* Now I would like to concentrate on the positives.

The Mindset for Success

Whether you decide to continue on your road up the corporate ladder or to become an entrepreneur, it's important that you always remember the *Laws of the Universe* and to also develop the mindset for success that most successful people have as their foundations.

Rich habit researcher Tom Corley has found differences between those who are rich and those who struggle to get by. The majority of wealthy people do the following, while only a small percentage of those who are poor do these things:

- 80% of wealthy people are focused on accomplishing a single goal
- 67% of wealthy people write down their goals

- 76% of wealthy people exercise aerobically 4 days a week

- 63% of wealthy people listen to educational audio books regularly

- 81% of wealthy people maintain a to-do list

- 67% of wealthy people watch 1 hour or less of TV every day

- 44% of wealthy people wake up 3 hours before work starts

- 84% of wealthy people believe good habits create opportunity

- 74% of wealthy people teach good daily success habits to their children

- **86% of wealthy people believe in life-long educational self-improvement vs. 5% for poor.**

Slowly re-read the list and then tick off the ones that you're doing on a daily basis. If you're life is not where you desire it to be, start to introduce these habits into your life. Remember you *are the only person you will spend your entire life* with and now you have 10 easy-to-implement habits that will create an enormous difference toward you being *joyous, prosperous and harmonious*.

Before we continue to our Global Purpose

I guess there really is only one way to end our discussion on Professional Purpose and to conclude a chapter titled "Working girl" and that is to reflect upon Tess McGill's (Melanie Griffith) classic line from the 1988 movie:

"No, I'm trying to make it better! I'm not gonna spend the rest of my life working my ass off and getting nowhere just because I followed rules that I had nothing to do with setting up, Ok?"

It's interesting to note that in 1988 women were also yearning for a life in which they could Be, Create and Collaborate, and in 2014 we are still yearning for the same thing.

Why in over a quarter of a century have we (women) not progressed leaps and bounds in advancing ourselves like we have in technology?

No wonder I am so passionate about the BraveHeart Women Global Community. Time to stop yearning ladies and start empowering yourself, as only you can:

> *Be* the person you came here to Be
>
> *Create* your prosperity with Ease
>
> *Collaborate* Harmoniously

Chapter Eight

We're Here to Serve

"Real success is not on the stage, but off the stage as a human being, and how you get along with your fellow man."

~ *Sammy Davis Jr.*

The last two chapters have assisted us on our journey; highlighting our first two purposes. Firstly our Personal Purpose, allowing us to *Blossom* into the people we came here to *Be,* and secondly our Professional Purpose, where we can *Create* our prosperity with Ease.

It is now time to look at our third and final purpose—our Global Purpose, which is for us to *Collaborate* harmoniously.

As I mentioned earlier, for most of my life I have been searching for my purposes, always thought there must be more to life. I loved the movie the Matrix, mainly because it confirmed for me what I have felt more or less all of my life, i.e. that we are all here playing a role, a movie role. That is right; we are the Director of our own lives.

We chose our parents, our siblings, our friends, some of the challenges we would face, though most importantly, who we would be and what our purpose was for coming to earth at this time and place.

I can never remember not feeling this way, though I am sure there was a time when I did not have such clarity, such knowing.

In early 2002, one of my sisters, Pam, gave me Sylvia Browne's *Life on the Other Side* book to read. Basically, it's a psychic's tour of the afterlife. I loved this book. It answered a lot of my questions. Whenever I heard of a friend or colleague who was dying, I would give them this book. I would say, "Read this, it will help you to live the rest of this life without fear, so you can more easily pass to your next adventure."

When my son Dan suddenly passed in 2011, I purchased 20 copies of the book. I re-read it myself to guide me through what was happening to Dan. It was a great help with the grieving process. I gave copies to many others, who were grateful as they also were not coping well with his sudden passing.

Whether we believe in the next life or not, it really does not matter. We are here now, living our lives as human beings and I love the ethos that we're *"spiritual beings having an earthly experience."*

Our Global Purpose is to *evolve, shift and contribute* to our fellow humans and also to our amazing planet.

In other words, we are here to *Serve*.

Many may misinterpret this to mean that we are here to give away all our worldly goods and become missionaries. This way of thinking is not serving you; as what serves and honours you, serves and honours others.

We are all here to have a joyous, prosperous and harmonious life whilst we are in service to our fellow humans.

Our ability to make more money is directly aligned with the number of people we can serve. If we're not making much money, we're also not helping many people. It's virtually impossible to help a greater number of people while remaining broke.

Money is symbolic of how we are growing and believing in ourselves.

Now is the time to start trusting that having more money is part of our spiritual path. Above all, begin trusting yourself.

BraveHeart Women's global purpose is to create harmony in the world. We believe this will happen through inspiring women to collaborate with other women. For us to come "through the heart without the mind", so we can move from competition to collaboration.

Some may argue that most of the conflicts in the world are due to MEN, their egos, trying to force everyone's beliefs and culture onto other people. We at BraveHeart Women believe that these conflicts are a symptom, not the cause.

The cause is actually women not being in Ease. When women are in Ease, in their Essence, men will follow. The old adage *"happy wife, happy life"* is so true.

When a woman has her self-esteem, everything falls into place. She begins to create the joyous, prosperous, harmonious life she desires. And when she is in harmony, so is her family.

And then a chain reaction begins to happen. Other women start to want what she has, they become inspired to empower themselves as she did. Then their family reaps the benefits, and then the whole street starts to take notice, and then the community, and then the country and then the whole world will be living in harmony.

It really is that simple. Our Global Purpose is to Collaborate and bring Harmony. And this begins by us all *"Being the change you want for the world."*

A couple of months ago I received an email from Marie-Jean, a friend who initially connected with me via LinkedIn. I would like to share some of Marie-Jean's initial email as this really resonated with me and our global purpose:

".... I haven't had any great female career contacts and have realised that it was missing in my life only this year. So I am making a conscious effort to connect to people such as yourself because I am finally in a position where I can help other females.

Truth be told, early on in my career, twice I had two female managers and it was the worst experience. I spent the next 15 years working only in male dominated workplaces. I now want to change that and help others.

I don't want to be like the managers I experienced early on and it would be wonderful to know I helped change a workplace..."

Marie-Jean truly understands the value in women collaborating. I am blessed to have her share this journey with me.

Can you imagine what it would be like to live in a world where we all collaborate? Allowing everyone to be who they are, believe what they want, live how they like? All they have to do is to co-habitat with their fellow human, so we all can live *a joyous, prosperous and harmonious life?*

Sounds delicious ... and it all begins by us, ladies, looking at a lady who is in her Essence, living her life in Ease and realising *"I want what she has"*.

From there, we will follow her example and become the example for others to follow.

All it takes is one person to start the chain reaction. There is a shift that is required, and don't you feel now is the time for us to evolve so we can contribute to this becoming a reality?

When we align with who we truly are, and expand our presence in the world, success naturally flows in abundance to us.

Are you ready to Evolve, Shift and Contribute?

Yes?

A good place to start is by completing the spaces in this statement as you so desire.

> *I am evolving into........................,*
>
> *as I hold the space to shift...................*
>
> *while contributing.......................*

Sit for a while contemplating how you may complete this statement. Allow your "heart energy" to give you the words. Intuitively you know the answer; you just may require a moment so you can quiet down your mind and let the answers flow to you.

Take your time. I have completed this statement several times. Once we start to evolve, it's continual. That is the beauty of being so conscious. We are continually evolving into our higher selves.

I now know that my life purpose is to be in service and through helping women achieve what they want, I will receive what I want—a joyous, prosperous and harmonious life.

My personal Global Purpose is to inspire young teenage mothers to *Blossom* into the women they came here to Be. Even though I never lived as an unmarried teenage mother, I certainly have a connection with these women.

In Australia, we have a social security system that unfortunately has allowed some people to have never worked in their life. We call the payments they receive the "dole". I am very passionate about inspiring these young mothers to see:

1. Self esteem is the key to our life, and putting ourselves first is not selfish.

2. We can still achieve all our life dreams whilst bringing up our children.

3. We'll never thrive whilst we are on social security.

My *"teenage mothers"* Global Purpose statement is:

I am evolving into **a woman visionary, releasing the fear of being judged**, as I hold the space to shift **the mindset of young teenage mothers in order for them to**

have self-esteem, so they can become everything they desire to Be, while contributing ***time and space as I nurture my vision.***

The reason teenage mothers are my Global Purpose and not my Professional Purpose is that I will give back to teenage mothers. My plan is to develop programs and scholarships so they can receive the tools to more easily Blossom into the women they came here to Be. That will allow them to Evolve, Shift and Contribute.

Our Planet

This book is all about our journey to becoming our own best friend, and as the planet sustains us, I thought I would briefly touch on ways that we can all assist in healing our planet.

Our planet is referred to as "Mother Earth", which is exactly what the planet was to all the million of species that call earth home. Like any mother, the Earth has fed us, clothed us, watered us, provided shelter, nurtured and allowed us to develop into the people and planet we are today.

Though our planet is now not well. It is time for us to give back, for us to nurture the planet, so maybe we shall change the name to "baby earth."

As Stephen Emmott stated in his book *Ten Billion***:**

We got to where we are now through a number of civilisation- and society-shaping "events", most notably the agricultural revolution, the scientific revolution, the industrial revolution and – in the West – the public-

health revolution.

Our emissions of CO2 modify our atmosphere. Our increasing water use had started to modify our hydrosphere. Rising atmospheric and sea-surface temperature had started to modify the cryosphere, most notably in the unexpected shrinking of the Arctic and Greenland ice sheets. Our increasing use of land, for agriculture, cities, roads, mining – as well as all the pollution we were creating – had started to modify our biosphere. Or, to put it another way: we had started to change our climate.

Whether you believe in climate change or not, there are simple and easy things we can introduce into our lives that make a difference every day, at home and at work.

By reducing our emissions of greenhouse gases we contribute to reducing the world's contribution to climate change, while sending a strong message to our government.

- **Electricity**: Reduce our greenhouse gas impact by purchasing some or all our energy from accredited *Green Power* suppliers. Also switch appliances off, purchase high energy-saving electrical equipment, use clothes washers and dryers with full loads.

- **Water:** Reduce our use of water, fix dripping taps. Don't buy bottled water.

- **Transport:** Look at alternative means of transportation. Car pool, drive smart, keep our cars serviced to reduce emissions.

- **Shopping**: *Buy less, waste less and choose products that last.* Choose goods that are organic and fresh. Choose products that are less likely to generate waste – reusable rather than disposable or made of recyclable materials.

Now is the time to *"Wake us up"* so we can step up and deliberately create a better, more conscious planet – a planet where we come together and serve and support one another as a whole – with our whole selves.

Chapter Nine

The Essence of a Global Community

"Life is like a camera, **Focus** *on what's important,* **Capture** *the good times.* **Develop** *from the negatives, and if things don't work out,* **Take** *another shot."*

~ *Unknown*

Before we continue, let's touch on a couple of reality points: *Life doesn't come with a guidebook* and our *Birth certificate does not have an expiry date on it.*

We don't have a roadmap and we don't know how much time we have to get what we want out of life. A good starting place is to Become our own Best Friend, and a good time to do that is now. Therein lies the solution to fulfilling the three things most people are looking for in their lives:

- More time

- More money

- More quality relationships

This book has highlighted all the things—our innate abilities, limiting beliefs, survival patterns, our lack of voice, our low self-esteem, our relationships with other women and much, much more—that we put in our way that stops us from becoming the person we desire to be.

But what if we could make some major changes to our lives, just by following an easy step-by-step plan?

Every day, we make a choice to step up or stay where we are. We can choose to be bold and live outside our comfort zone despite our fears, or we can stay in our comfort zone and play it safe. Unfortunately, the more we live inside our comfort zone, the less comfortable it becomes. Eventually, our comfort zone will become uncomfortable…very uncomfortable.

So let's revisit the four major fears that we all have that are keeping us in our comfort zones:

- Fear of abandonment
- Fear of not doing enough
- Fear of not feeling safe
- Fear of losing control

And the rule to changing anything in our life is:

1. To Be aware

2. And to Be aware that I am aware that I have …….

3. And to Smile often

Making us aware of the things that have been holding us back is the Essence of this book. Let's look at an example of how to use the *three ways to change anything*.

In this case, we'll look at an issue that a lot of women struggle with – *the fear of rejection.* This ties back to *Fear of Abandonment*, especially in a sales environment.

Women are funny creatures:

- We do not want to sell (give me any job except a sales job)
- We do not want to be sold to, especially if it's a woman doing the selling

- Though we love to buy!!

Yes we have all this wrapped up in side of us.

Ok, back to the example on how we can work through and solve this fear:

Step 1: I become aware that I have a *fear of rejection*.

Step 2: I step out and look at myself with a *fear of rejection*

Step 3: Then I grin quietly to myself, knowing that the *fear of rejection* is just a belief that I have been holding. It does not have any true weight to it.

Be here now. Do not think about the last phone call in which you were rejected. Instead, think:

"I am not predicting a rejection for my next call and I'll just stay here in the present. I enjoy this call as an opportunity to connect with another human being. It's just an opportunity to express myself and BE myself."

Be present in the moment. This is the Key. A fear can only arise by predicting something or remembering something. If you are not predicting and you are not remembering and you are here now, then fear doesn't exist.

Fear can be debilitating and it's the major reason we cannot fulfill the six basic needs we all have as humans:

1. Need of certainty

2. Need for variety

3. Need for the feeling of significance

4. Need for connection or love

5. Need for growth

6. Need for contribution

Now is the time, for us to fulfill all our basic needs ... Now is the time to step outside our comfort zones and create the life we desire. And let's face it, you're obviously looking for something or you would not be reading this book. None of us want to have any regrets when we do pass to the other side.

Bronnie Ware, an Australian nurse who spent several years working in palliative care for patients in the last 12 weeks of their lives, wrote a book titled, *The Top Five Regrets of the Dying*. Here they are, as witnessed by Ware:

> 1. *I wish I'd had the courage to live a life true to myself, not the life others expected of me.* "This was the most common regret of all. When people realise that their life is almost over and look back clearly on it, it is easy to see how many dreams have gone unfulfilled. Most people had not honoured even a half of their dreams and had to die knowing that it was due to choices they had made, or not made. Health brings a freedom very few realise, until they no longer have it."

2. *I wish I hadn't worked so hard.* "This came from every male patient that I nursed. They missed their children's youth and their partner's companionship. Women also spoke of this regret, but as most were from an older generation, many of the female patients had not been breadwinners. All of the men I nursed deeply regretted spending so much of their lives on the treadmill of a work existence."

3. *I wish I'd had the courage to express my feelings.* "Many people suppressed their feelings in order to keep peace with others. As a result, they settled for a mediocre existence and never became who they were truly capable of becoming. Many developed illnesses relating to the bitterness and resentment they carried as a result."

4. *I wish I had stayed in touch with my friends.* "Often they would not truly realise the full benefits of old friends until their dying weeks and it was not always possible to track them down. Many had become so caught up in their own lives that they had let golden friendships slip by over the years. There were many deep regrets about not giving friendships the time and effort that they deserved. Everyone misses their friends when they are dying."

5. *I wish that I had let myself be happier.* "This is a surprisingly common one. Many did not realise until the end that happiness is a choice. They had stayed stuck in old patterns and habits. The so-called 'comfort' of familiarity overflowed into their emotions, as well as their physical lives.

Fear of change had them pretending to others, and to their selves, that they were content, when deep within, they longed to laugh properly and have silliness in their life again."

What's your greatest regret so far? And what will you set out to achieve or change before you die?

Only *you* can make the choice to learn, grow and continually be better than you were yesterday.

A solution lies within you taking another journey, a journey that will give you a *quantum leap* into becoming the person you are yearning to be, so when you do eventually pass, you will have fulfilled every desire you have ever thought about and will have no regrets.

BraveHeart Women and the Quantum Journey

BraveHeart Women offers a new way for women to be with themselves and with each other. As we have discussed earlier, the old paradigm has always been based in patriarchal values that foster competition, jealousy, distrust and sometimes meanness amongst women.

The new feminine model is about learning first how to Be, living in your Essence, then learning how to Create your prosperity with ease and Collaborate with other women. This model supports a true bonding and friendship between women of all ages, nationalities and backgrounds. Collaboration is the name of the game at BraveHeart Women.

The BraveHeart Women community offers many new

ways for women to open more to their intuition and listen to their heart rather than their brain.

Living from your heart, being transparent, living in the moment, being spontaneous and embodying Ease and grace. BraveHeart Women are committed to supporting women in becoming financially prosperous and in living their visions; in other words, to *"become their own best friend, who is joyous, prosperous and harmonious."*

I love the person I have become, since travelling to Los Angeles with my friend and colleague, Kaz Pearce, to attend *Rise LA 2012*, the annual four-day BraveHeart Women conference.

I sat there for four days listening to Ellie Drake, the inspirational founder, nodding my head in agreement to everything Ellie shared with us.

I had never heard most of the information before, though I intuitively knew that everything she shared was correct. So much so that when I was told that I could open a chapter in my local area, I raised my hand immediately. It was my big **AHA moment**, "Aha that is why I was made redundant in my CFO role. *This is my purpose. Always had the voice, never the message. Now my voice is content.*"

During the past two years, I've attended numerous trainings that convinced me even more – my purpose is to bring these tools to Australian women. In reality, it's to bring them to all women, all over the globe, hence I am writing this book.

Though my BraveHeart Women community chapters and trainings are run here in Australia, there are many other BraveHeart Women worldwide bringing the tools and trainings to women in their local areas.

That is the beauty of being part of a global community.

We share the tools and information in many formats, via chapter meetings, webinars, Skype calls, daily events and three-day events.

The Female Quantum Journey curriculum provides the content for our chapter meetings, webinars, talks and day programs. The webinar series is comprised of six individual classes that bundle together to create a powerful learning path, that's delivered to you over 29 weeks.

This is the key to you living your life in Essence, being your own best friend, so you can **Be, Create and Collaborate.**

The information you receive each week is enormous. We liken it to *"drinking out of a fire hydrant"*, so we have extended the training to include a group Q&A Skype call with others and six live day (chapter) meetings.

That way you receive the information three times, so you can absorb and embody everything, allowing you to reap the benefits immediately.

Let's look at the six individual classes that will help you get past some of the barriers that have been stopping you from creating the life you so desire.

1. **Barriers to the Female Success Model**

    a. Do you feel, in this moment, you have the vitality in every cell of your body you require to create abundant success?

    b. Do you feel you could move from Fight, Flight, or Freeze to operate from a state of Ease?

    c. Could you easily move from Survival to Thriving?

    d. Could you give birth to your super potential by igniting your *Personal Purpose, Professional Purpose and Global Purpose?*

2. **Barriers to Female Prosperity Model**

    a. Did you know that when we experience rejection as women we create energetic germs that attack what we call our prosperity system?

    b. Did you know we create disease in our mind and convince ourselves that it is not our goal to even create prosperity?

    c. Are you ready to learn to activate your prosperity energy centre, so you can move away from a Lack mindset?

    d. Are you ready to develop the skill of receiving, which will allow prosperity?

3. **Barriers to New Healer**

a. Your voice is the key to you tapping into the magnitude of the energy that resides in you.

b. Are you ready to own what you have been called to BE?

c. Everything in life resides around 2 things: To Choose or Not to Choose

d. Are you ready to shift everything into the Music of Your Voice?

4. **Female Business Model**

   a. Work as CEO of your business, even if you work for someone else you will develop this mindset, which will assist you to grow into a CEO.

   b. A mindset shift – creating in order to expand into a thriving pond:

   - Right People

   - You being the Director

   - CEO mindset – learn to delegate, leverage time energy & resource

   - Get out of your own way

   c. Bring tangible results

   d. Retain clients Enhance your brand – target an audience who cares

  e. Queen of conversions; Increased results; Marketing, conversion, conversation

5. **Female Revenue Model**

  a. Born Nurtured

  b. Outdated business formulas – old model = pain & scarcity

  c. Pleasure & Urgency

  d. Return on time – shift you out of the non-profit mindset

  e. Master the art of client relationships – be a preventer instead of a fixer.

6. **Female Sales Training**

  a. What is your perception?

  b. Learn to be a grounded artist. Master this art

  c. Express the value of your product

  d. Be able to communicate the value within the first couple of minutes

  e. Communicate the value in such a way that they tell you what they want.

The Quantum Journey series is available to anyone who registers. You do not have to be a BraveHeart Women chapter member to enrol.

Conclusion

I firmly believe that BraveHeart Women and the tools we provide is the key to every woman becoming their own best friend and living a *joyous, prosperous and harmonious fulfilled life.*

This global community is the key to us creating the world we all want to live in—a planet that is at peace, living in harmony with everyone, no matter our culture, religious beliefs or nationalities.

The beauty of the BraveHeart Women community is that you can have as little or as much as you like. You can be an online member, a chapter member, a DYBO (Dance Your But's Off) specialist, a DYBO participant, a person who comes to Rise conference every year, and/or you can become a Resonator, who opens up her own chapter in her area.

Yes, a Resonator, don't you just love the word? We are not just facilitators, we are **Resonators**, as everything we share Resonates with us and people like us.

Totally amazing. Are you ready to BE, CREATE, and COLLABORATE?

Yes? Fantastic, then I look forward to you coming on this journey with me. It's a journey that will help you move away from:

- *Ego to **Essence***
- *Personal will to **Divine Will***

- Competition to **Collaboration**

- Reactivity to **Neutrality**
- Lack to **Prosperity**

- Sympathy to **Empathy**

- Repression to **Expression**

- Mental mind to **Intuitive Mind**

- Mentor to **Example**

I invite you to check out the BraveHeart website. You can join for free and take a look around.

If you are a woman like me who is committed to creating and supporting the new feminine paradigm, then Braveheart Women is a wonderful place to align and meet other women who feel the same way.

Go to **www.bravheartwomen.com**, fill in your details and in the space titled *"Who invited you"*, please type *Karen Chaston*.

You might also want to check out our Rise website, **www.risela.com** about our annual four-day conference in Los Angeles. Email me if you are interested in coming along one year. I am sure I will be able to organise a discounted ticket for you.

Kaz and I are very passionate about providing many ways for women to receive these tools so they can Blossom into the person they came here to *Be*, *Create* their prosperity with Ease and *Collaborate* harmoniously.

We provide these trainings on a personal basis (chapter meetings) as well as in the workplace, where we specially design the content that best suits the company's requirements for their women and their workplace.

And if you would like more details about the best way for you to quantum journey into becoming your own best friend, go to my website or email me.

I would love to hear your story, the first step in us getting to know each other.
karen.chaston@braveheartwomenresonate.com

Thank you for coming on this journey with me. I trust you have enjoyed it as much as I have enjoying writing this for you. I look forward to our paths crossing again.

Be well until we connect again.

With Love and Joy,

Karen Chaston
A BraveHeart Woman who Resonates
www.karenchaston.com.au
karen.chaston@braveheartwomenresonate.com

Afterword

It would have been remiss of me to not include these last couple of thoughts for you to reflect upon.

Firstly, I mentioned earlier that I was never one to hang out with the girls. I also found it easier to hang with the guys. This is no longer the case. Don't get me wrong, I love to spend time with my husband, Andrew, sons Ben and Josh, and all the other men in my life. Though now, the majority of my time I am with women.

And I can honestly say I love being a woman.

I also love listening to Beyonce's song "If I Were A Boy". It highlights why we stay true to who we are as women. (Here is a link to an awesome clip Beyonce starred in:
https://www.youtube.com/watch?v=AWpsOqh8q0M)

Lastly, I am borrowing the Afterword from the book *Dying to Be Me* by Anita Moorjani (another book I highly recommend you read) for us all to enjoy, embrace and reflect upon. This sums up so beautifully what I have been trying to portray.

> *Before I close, I'd like to leave you with a few final words. Always remember not to give away your power-instead, get in touch with your own magnificence. When it comes to finding the right path, there's a different answer for each person. The only universal solution I have is to love yourself unconditionally and be yourself fearlessly!*
>
> *This is the most important lesson I have learned from my N.D.E.[Near Death Experience], and I honestly feel if I'd known this, I would never would*

have gotten cancer in the first place.
When we're true to ourselves, we become instruments of truth for the planet. Because we are all connected, we touch the lives of everyone around us, who then affect others. Our only obligation is to be the love we are and allow our answers to come from within in the way that's most appropriate for us.

Finally, I can't stress enough how important it is to enjoy yourself and not take yourself or life too seriously. One of the biggest flaws with many traditional spiritual systems is that they often make us take life too seriously. Although you know that I abhor creating doctrines, if I ever had to create a set of tenets for a spiritual path to healing my number one on my list would be to make sure to laugh as often as possible, throughout every single day - and preferably laugh at myself. This would be hands down over and above any form of prayer, meditation, and chanting or diet reform. Day-to-day problems never seem as big when viewed through a veil of humour and love.

In the age of information technology, we're bombarded with news seemingly at the speed of light. We're living in an age of high stress and fear, and in the midst of trying to protect ourselves from everything we think is 'out there', we're forgotten to enjoy ourselves and to take care of what's inside.

Our life is our prayer. It's our gift to this universe, and the memories we leave behind when we someday exit this world will be our legacy to our loved ones. We owe it to ourselves and to everyone around us to be happy and to spread that Joy around.

If we go through life armed with humour and the realisation that we are love, we'll already be ahead of the game. Add a box of chocolates into the mix, and we've really got a winning formula!

I wish you Joy as you realise your magnificence and express yourself fearlessly in the world.

Be well until we connect again.

With Love and Joy,

References

"Accustom yourself not to be disregarding of what someone else has to say: as far as possible enter into the mind of the speaker."

~ *Marcus Aurelius, Meditations*

Every book, audio, blog, song, quote, training, talk, conference and conversation I have experienced during my life were in my heart and head as I wrote this book. I had the pleasure of listening to Seth Godin (American author, entrepreneur, marketer, and public speaker) speak and he so eloquently described the new age world we live in, *"every fact in the world is three clicks away."* This is so true, I have merely brought these facts together and arranged them around my life story, in order to inspire and assist you to easily journey toward discovering your unique self. Below are the direct references I have integrated into this book, *A Journey to Becoming Your Own Best Friend.*

Books

Social psychologist Susan Newman's *The Book of No*

Norma J Milanovich and Shirley D McCunes' book *The Light Shall Set You Free*

Deepak Chopra's *Seven Spiritual Signs of Success*

Stephen Emmott's *Ten Billion*

Bronnie Ware's *The Top Five Regrets of the Dying*

Anita Moorjani's *Dying to Be Me*

Dr. Wayne Dyer, *Don't die with the music, still inside of you*

Stories compiled by Christine Kloser, Lynne Klippel and Michael Port in *Align, Expand and Succeed*

Songs

Beyonce's song "If I Were a Boy…"
https://www.youtube.com/watch?v=AWpsOqh8q0M

Jason Mraz song "I Won't Give Up"..**https://www.youtube.com/watch?v=boWUsQwdet4**

Reference sites

Comparison of Empathy and Sympathy from:
http://www.diffen.com/difference/Empathy_vs_Sympathy

http://dictionary.reference.com/help/faq/language/d23.html

Trainings

BraveHeart Women Global Community Resonator training programs

About the Author

Karen Chaston is a wife, mother, author and former Chief Financial Officer (CFO) of a publicly listed company, who knows first-hand what adrenalin (or specifically stress), does to a woman's body.

Karen is also a BraveHeart Women Resonator at BraveHeart Women Global Community, an established community that inspires women to Be more, Create more and Collaborate more. She brought the BraveHeart Women community to Australia in 2013 and is focused on creating brand awareness, building chapter membership around Sydney, and assisting more Australian Resonators in building their own chapters.

With a wealth of knowledge and experience amassed over the course of an illustrious 20-year career in leadership and business, Karen strives for excellence in her every endeavour and seeks to expand an ever-growing network.

Karen's vision is to help women in a corporate, business and professional background to rediscover and utilise their natural intuitive abilities and to realise how powerful and fulfilling it can be to live this way.

Her passion is to collaborate in creating a new world for generations to come—one with more "conscious entrepreneurs" who allow their *hearts and souls,* along with their *knowledge and expertise*, to guide their businesses.

Karen lives on the northern beaches, Sydney, Australia with her husband of more than 36 years, Andrew and their dog Sirius, a male spoodle.

For more information: **www.karenchaston.com.au**

www.ingramcontent.com/pod-product-compliance
Lightning Source LLC
Chambersburg PA
CBHW060525090426
42735CB00011B/2371